Decolonizing Politics

Decolonizing the Curriculum series

Ali Meghji, *Decolonizing Sociology*

Decolonizing Politics

An Introduction

Robbie Shilliam

polity

First published in 2021 by Polity Press

Polity Press
65 Bridge Street
Cambridge CB2 1UR, UK

Polity Press
101 Station Landing
Suite 300
Medford, MA 02155, USA

ISBN-13: 978-1-5095-3938-3 (hardback)
ISBN-13: 978-1-5095-3939-0 (paperback)

A catalogue record for this book is available from the British Library.

Library of Congress Cataloging-in-Publication Data
Names: Shilliam, Robbie, 1969- author.
Title: Decolonizing politics : an introduction / Robbie Shilliam.
Description: Cambridge, UK ; Medford, MA : Polity Press, 2021. | Series: Decolonizing the curriculum | Includes bibliographical references and index. | Summary: "An ideal student primer exploring why, and how, the study of politics should be decolonized"-- Provided by publisher.
Identifiers: LCCN 2020037765 (print) | LCCN 2020037766 (ebook) | ISBN 9781509539383 (hardback) | ISBN 9781509539390 (paperback) | ISBN 9781509539406 (epub)
Subjects: LCSH: Political science--Philosophy. | Political participation. | Comparative government. | International relations.
Classification: LCC JA71 .S444 2021 (print) | LCC JA71 (ebook) | DDC 320.01--dc23
LC record available at https://lccn.loc.gov/2020037765
LC ebook record available at https://lccn.loc.gov/2020037766

Typeset in 10.5 on 12.5pt Sabon
by Fakenham Prepress Solutions, Fakenham, Norfolk NR21 8NL
Printed and bound in Great Britain by CPI Group (UK) Ltd, Croydon

For further information on Polity, visit our website:
politybooks.com

For Kōkiri and Reremoana. And to all the children who must find ways over, under, around, and through wicked Babylon.

Contents

Acknowledgments

My thanks to Jacob Kripp, Stephanie Najjar, Nandini Dey, and Sheharyar Imran for their help. Thanks also to Inès Boxman, Sophie Wright, and Louise Knight at Polity for all their support. And thanks to two anonymous reviewers for their useful comments.

–1–

Introduction

Let's start with a figure who is conventionally known as the "father" of political science – Aristotle. You might think this strange for a book that seeks to decolonize the study of politics: isn't Aristotle a very Eurocentric departure point? Not if you asked Aristotle. He categorized Europeans as barbarians. Paul Cartledge (1993, 5), an eminent historian of the classical world, describes the ancient Greeks as "desperately foreign" to our Western sensibilities. Or how about Derek Walcott, famous Saint Lucian poet and Nobel Prize winner, who compares the Aegean and Caribbean seas and finds much in common:

> If we looked at them now, we would say that the Greeks had Puerto Rican tastes. Right? Because the stones were painted brightly. They were not these bleached stones. Time went by, and they sort of whitened and weathered, the classics began to be thought of as something bleached-out and rain-spotted, distant. (Brown and Johnson 1996, 183).

Perhaps Aristotle is not so much a strange departure point as an uncanny one. Investigating the place of aboriginal ideas of the sacred in mainstream Australian society, Ken

Gelder and Jane Jacobs (1995, 171) define the uncanny as "the combination of the familiar and the unfamiliar – the way the one seems always to *inhabit* the other." Aristotle is familiar: we are used to conceiving of him as the progenitor of a European science of politics. Yet he is also unfamiliar: in fact, Aristotle was *not* European, so what does that make of the purportedly European tradition of studying politics?

Facing the uncanny unsettles our assumptions in an intimate fashion. Intimacy is important. There's an easy option to decolonizing the study of politics. You can simply search for the most exotic forms of politics around the world and revel in their alien-ness. But in doing so, you'd keep the "familiar" familiar and the "unfamiliar" unfamiliar. There would be no intimate engagement there between "them" and "us." No question raised as to what counts as "exotic' to whom and why. No stakes at play.

Put another way, if you moved your focus to a study of the "margins" only, then that would leave the "center" intact. Your movement would thereby avoid difficult but compelling questions such as: Who made their lives central and other peoples' lives marginal? And, by what logics are the margins divided from the center? There are many different kinds of centers and margins. In this book we are going to focus on imperial centers and colonial margins. We will be decolonizing the study of politics by rethinking both these centers and margins; but to do that we will have to take marginalized perspectives seriously.

Empirically, imperialism pertains to the expansion of a polity's influence or dominion through usually militaristic but also economic and diplomatic means. Imperial administration is a hierarchical affair, with a center that is served by a diverse set of peripheries. Imperialism is mostly a violent affair in so far as it forces the center of some peoples' worlds to become the margins of another people's world. Colonialism is principally about governing those marginal populations. Such governance can take many forms. I will draw attention to two here. Firstly, there is an indirect kind of colonial rule whereby a small coterie of foreign administrators (usually from the imperial center) appoint indigenous "chiefs" to rule over "tribes" on their behalf. Think of Ghana. The second version is where populations from the imperial center colonize and settle lands and govern themselves while also ruling over indigenous peoples. In this instance, settlers often become the majority due to land dispossession and other techniques of genocide. Think of New Zealand.

You might say that empires and colonies no longer exist. A few colonies still do, but let me grant the point. However, the claim I will make in this book is that political science remains indebted to approaches, debates and categories that emerged to make sense of the challenges that imperial centers faced in ruling over the colonial margins that they had created. In this respect, empire and colonialism are formative phenomena in the study of politics. Case in point: our uncanny Aristotle, who was born into a colonial world.

Aristotle's World

Aristotle was born in Stagiera, a typical Greek colony-city. Before the wars with Persia (499–450 BCE), it was commonplace for Greek cities to send out settlers to found new cities. The hundreds of small autonomous cities produced in this colonizing movement provided the lattice of Greek politics. For instance, Aristotle's mother came from Chalcis. Chalcis and another city, Andros, together sponsored the settlement of Stagiera almost 300 years before Aristotle's birth in 384 BCE. You've no doubt heard of Aristotle's ideal model for a political community. Well, his description of the "polis" – its shape, size and substance – was remarkably similar to the colony-city of his birth.

Let's be under no illusion: Greek colonization – like all colonization – was a conflictual and often bloody process. Nonetheless, in the "archaic" period (the hundreds of years before the Persian Wars) Greeks colonized in a manner similar to most groups of people who inhabited the shores of the Mediterranean. Greeks were all too aware that they shared these ancient shores with empires to the Asian east and African south – empires that were often older, wealthier, and more powerful than them. Therefore, although colonizers themselves, Greeks did not necessarily consider themselves to be superior beings. Their settlers did not even feel the compulsion to eradicate the foreign gods of the lands that they colonized. Such gods were mapped onto figures that already comprised the Greek pantheon; either that, or their pantheon received new members.

One of the ways by which Greeks oriented themselves to this world of colonies and empires was by contrasting themselves to "barbarians." You're probably thinking about the derogatory nature of this term. Actually, in the archaic era "barbarian" straightforwardly referred to a non-Greek speaker. How about xenophobia? You'll be aware of the hatred of foreigners usually implied by that term. But in the archaic era, "xenoi" referred to a "guest-friend" (see Malkin 2004). Evidently, the Greeks did not think themselves as fundamentally superior to the multicultural empires with which they shared the Mediterranean.

All this changed during the Persian Wars. Athens rose to become the hegemon of the Delian league, a collection of Greek cities that faced the imperial armies and navies of the Persian empire. As these autonomous cities came increasingly under Athenian rule, so were their distinctive identities sidelined by a new cultural identity of imperial belonging: Hellenism. At the same time, "barbarian" came to be associated primarily with Persians, who were described as a sensual and effeminate race of men. "Hellenic" thus came to reference a superior masculine civilization to the lesser barbarians that threatened it.

But the consolidation of imperial power by Athens invited challenge beyond the Persians. Macedonians, who lived north of Mount Olympus, spoke a Greek dialect and worshiped gods from the Greek pantheon. They were, though, considered by Greeks to be barbarians. Regardless, by the time Aristotle was born, the imperial designs of Macedonia also began to threaten Athens and its leadership of the Delian league. As it happens, Aristotle's father served as a court physician to the Macedonian king Amyntas II during his short reign. Aristotle himself most likely spent some of his early childhood in the

Macedonian palace at Pella. These connections would cause persistent trouble for him in later life.

So, Aristotle was born into a colonial world increasingly shaped by inter-imperial competition. On his mother's side he inherited the Greek settler project of founding independent colony-cities. On his father's side he inherited a connection to the court of an expansionary imperial power.

That said, much of Aristotle's own life would be spent in Athens as an immigrant, or what we would nowadays call a "permanent alien" or "permanent resident." James Watson (2010) helpfully points out that the Greek term for immigrant – metic – originally referred to a person who changed his dwelling from one land to another. In the archaic period, before Athenian hegemony and when distinctions between Greeks and non-Greeks were less fraught, metic women could marry Athenian men and their children would become Athenian citizens. Even during the war with Persia thousands of people arrived in Athens fleeing military invasion and most subsequently gained citizenship. But all this changed when Athens won the war under the leadership of Pericles.

In 451 BCE Pericles introduced a law that limited the conferring of citizenship only to children of two Athenian parents. Effectively, the law ruled out the granting of citizenship to immigrants. With this, the status of metic was drastically redefined. True, unlike slaves – and most households had them in Athens – metics were at least free. Nevertheless, metics could not own land, vote in the assembly, serve as a magistrate, or represent themselves in court without a sponsor. Unlike citizens, metics had to pay a poll tax and failure to do so could lead to enslavement. Despite this inequity, metics had the same obligations as citizens to serve in the army and navy. After the end of the Persian war, approximately one third to one half of the free population in Athens were metics.

At the age of seventeen, Aristotle moved to Athens and there attended Plato's academy for nineteen years. Aristotle's experiences in Athens were defined by his metic status. For instance, when setting up his own school in the Lyceum area of Athens, Aristotle could not buy land but had to rent the property. He even confided to a friend that "the same things are not proper for a foreigner as they are for a citizen: it is difficult to stay in Athens" (Anagnostopoulos 2009, 9). Tellingly, in his writings Aristotle often referred to Athenians as "they" rather than as "us" (Dietz 2012, 284).

In fact, Aristotle was cast more than once as an anti-Athenian self-hating Greek sympathizer of Macedonia. Anti-Macedonian sentiment intensified when, under Philip II's command, the Macedonian army began expanding into the territories of the Delian league, which were under Athenian leadership. Soon after Plato's death, Aristotle left Athens under some duress. It seems as if some Athenians resented his familial connections to Macedonia. Return to Stagiera was not wise; Aristotle's birthplace had recently been destroyed by Philip II and its residents sent into exile or sold into slavery. Instead, Aristotle was welcomed to Atarnesu, a settler-city on the coast of Asia Minor (in present-day Turkey), by an old student of Plato. Having married his wife Pythias there, Aristotle moved the family to the island of Lesbos.

In 342, Philip II invited Aristotle to tutor his son, the future Alexander the Great. Aristotle returned to the palace at Pella for two years, introducing the young Alexander to the study of politics and writing for him two works on the subjects of monarchy and colonies. Thereafter, Aristotle journeyed home to Stagiera in time to witness the conquering of Athens by Philip II and the formation of a new federation of Greek cities – the League of Corinth – under Philip's influence.

After Philip's assassination and the ascent of his son Alexander, Aristotle returned to Athens for a second stay, during which he wrote his most influential treatise on the study of politics. He did, though, keep his Macedonian associations, including a friendship with Antipater, Alexander's viceroy, who held supreme command over the League of Corinth. After Alexander's untimely death, and with anti-Macedonian sentiment again sweeping through Athens, Aristotle left Athens for the last time. He retired to Chalcis, the colony-city where his mother's family held estates, and died there soon after.

Is not the political world of Aristotle uncanny to us? It is surely familiar in many ways: most present-day nations have colonial pasts; states across the world enact laws that make immigrants second class in comparison to first-class citizens; xenophobia easily sways political debate; and people flee wars to become asylum seekers and refugees. But it is also an unfamiliar world: we do not imagine colonial politics to play out in Greece, and Greece is supposed to be the ancient root of the European Union, not the center of non-European inter-imperial politics.

Above all, this uncanniness leads us to suspect that empire is an unexceptional political phenomenon. We might have to face the possibility that our foundational understandings of the political world are filtered through colonialism far more than we might imagine to be the case. Consider this. When he wrote his treatise on *Politics,* Aristotle had already moved from his original colony-city to become a permanent alien. He then effectively became an asylum seeker and subsequently moved between two imperial powers. Even if he was relatively privileged, Aristotle's life was also that of a sojourner, escapee, resident alien – not that of a settled, rights-holding, "native" citizen. Acknowledging this uncanniness allows us to re-orient toward Aristotle and his analysis of politics.

Many of the textbooks you might come across will introduce Aristotle as the first teacher of political science. Through his writings, you will be told, Aristotle proposed that man was a "political animal," that the nature of this animal was to seek out the "good life," that this life required systems of justice, and that the polis was the exemplary organization by which such normative aspirations could be met. Textbooks will also tell you that Aristotle described a wide array of political orders as well as the best methods by which to investigate and evaluate the actions of politicians and regimes.

Aristotle did cover this ground; no one is lying to you. But perhaps the problem lies in the ways in which textbooks condense Aristotle's study of politics to a framework centered upon the citizen of the polis. It goes something like this: the lawmaker crafts legislation, especially a constitution that preserves order over the various inhabitants of the polis; politicians govern through the laws, customs and educational institutions that uphold the constitution; and, in pursuit of the good life, citizens hold a right to participate in political deliberation.

To be fair, textbooks will often mention along the way the inadequacies of Athenian justice when it came to women, slaves, and barbarians. Sometimes a note of caution might be struck over Aristotle's apparent disdain for barbarians, his claim that some people are "natural slaves," and that women are inferior to men. But textbooks will still tend to separate Aristotle's "ideal" model from its "real" politics.

By the "ideal" I mean a framework that focuses on the citizen in relation to the polis, such that the logic of this relationship is self-sufficient and exclusive of imperial entanglements. By the "real," I mean the wider imperial and colonial contexts in and through which the very practice of citizenship gained meaning for Aristotle. Does this separation of the "ideal" and the "real" quell that unsettled feeling? Does it make Aristotle comfortably familiar again? I hope not.

Because in light of the contextualization we just undertook it seems conceptually inadequate to separate the polis from empire, and the non-citizen from citizen. The logic that Aristotle used to bind the citizen to the polis is not self-sufficient and exclusive of imperial entanglements. What if we started from the premises that Aristotle's polis was intractably modeled on the small settler-colony of his birth, and that his focus on democratic deliberation was at root an attempt to redress the harms of imperial expansion? (see Dietz 2012).

Don't get me wrong. I'm not claiming that Aristotle was what we nowadays call a "decolonizer" of political science. He wasn't even a revolutionary. He was conservative in the literal sense. That is, Aristotle wished to conserve the possibility of living in a just polis, but one that for him was modelled on the small settler-colony of his birth. Crucially, Aristotle believed that imperial expansion and the wars that served such expansion had radically curtailed that possibility. This was not only the case when it came to evaluating the barbarians of the Persian empire but also with regard to the trajectory of the Greek city leagues under the ambitions of both Athens and Macedonia (see, in general, Tuplin 1985). For Aristotle, empires by and large produced despots; and even citizens had to slavishly serve despots.

Aristotle's position could not have been a comfortable one from which to write a treatise on politics: he sought to dialogue with Athenian citizens, living among them, but not as one of them. Aristotle's philosophical provocation to them was something like this: "here is what you believe and practice; here is the logic to it; knowing this, do you think you should reappraise your beliefs and practices?" Indeed, his conception of politics itself was designed to address precisely such an intimately unsettling question.

Let's start with Aristotle's most famous statement: "a human is by nature a political animal" (Aristotle 2017, 4). But what does he mean by nature? As Jill Frank (2004) explains, nature for Aristotle signals "what happens usually and for the most part." The nature of humans can neither be accidental – which would make that nature inexplicable – nor defined in terms of necessities – which would make that nature unchangeable. Rather, nature is stable enough to be studied, but variable enough such that any study will be imperfect.

Naturally (usually and for the most part) we humans care for each other, whether that be through friendships or families (Salkever 2014, 71). What's more, says Aristotle, like most animals we are endowed with voluntary action, that is, we can choose to act. However, our capability to choose is a unique one. Unlike animals we can make choices by first using reason to evaluate all the possible courses of action (Aristotle 2014, 38–40).

If we put these concerns for sociability, agency, and reason together, then human nature can be explained in Aristotelian terms as a collective deliberation toward choosing the best course of action by which to attain the good life. Of course, such deliberation involves judgment. And for this reason, judgment is more of an art than a science, requiring practical wisdom, that is, insight applied to particular situations. For Aristotle (2014, 105–106), then, the study of politics cannot be simply the scientific analysis of universal laws but must always be a deliberative discussion about what might be best for the polity in any given time and place.

Still, deliberation requires leisure time and therein lies the rub. Those who plant the fields, raise children, clean households, and manufacture goods do not have any spare time. Therefore, politics can only be undertaken by virtue of a hierarchical division of labor that enfranchises some men as active citizens over and against other people in their household such as women, workers, slaves etc. Here we return to face Aristotle's conservatism, but in a different light: he wishes to preserve the hierarchical order of settler-colonies that makes politics, and thus the good life, possible.

Recall, though, Aristotle's understanding of nature as a condition that usually and in the main attains, and is neither random nor necessary. This understanding affects how he conceives of hierarchy. There is a subtle but important distinction between arguing that (a) hierarchy is *usual* and claiming that (b) certain peoples *by necessity and essence* occupy certain places in that hierarchy.

And think of all the paths that Aristotle has traveled in his life by the time he writes his *Politics*. He has moved from a citizen of a colony-city to a resident alien of another city, to a barbarian-sympathizer, to an asylum seeker, to an academic in the court of empire, and back to a resident alien again. All his life he has moved into and through different hierarchies. Given this lived experience of politics, it is reasonable to suppose that Aristotle is trying to sensitize Athenian citizens to the fact that the hierarchical world they live in is changeable. Citizens, too, might not be essentially superior to anyone else. The great can also degenerate.

Take, for instance, one of Aristotle's most infamous discussions concerning the "natural slave." As scholars such as Michael Heath (2008) have argued, what distinguishes the citizen from the slave for Aristotle is a very distinct and exacting condition: the practical inability to take part in deliberating on predetermined ends. Aristotle does not mean to imply that the slave is incapable of deliberation, which for him would be the case with a child. Rather, for most of the time and in most cases the slave cannot practically enter into deliberation with others in an independent manner.

Basically, the definition of a natural slave is what the citizen categorically is not. This is no surprise, given the fact that Aristotle's ideal for the household is a division between citizens and slaves. So long as that division enables citizens to take part actively in politics, that is, deliberation toward the good life, then slavery is ultimately a good thing. The peace and prosperity enjoyed by the master even trickles down to benefit his slave.

We'll return to these assumptions shortly. But why might Aristotle be making such an argument in his own context? If we refuted the assumption that certain people are essentially born slaves, then anyone might become a slave if the political system they inhabit practically forbids deliberation for the sake of the good life. And Aristotle defines slavery, you'll recall, as the opposite of citizenship. Consequently, imperial ambition, whether homegrown in Athens or imposed by Macedonia or Persia, might corrupt the polity, foreclose independent deliberation, and produce slavish citizens who must serve despots.

We can also think about the distinction between citizen and barbarian in like manner. Aristotle is influenced by earlier work that attributed the diversity of human capabilities to the effect upon semen production caused by climactic conditions. Yes, it is that graphic. In this model, as Julie Ward (2002) shows, the mild climate in Asia produces gentle, timid folk, while the cold climate in Europe produces wild, belligerent folk. As luck would have it, the Greek climate falls in between the two (Aristotle did not conceive of the Greeks as European) and so produces a balanced disposition of rationality and courage.

Are some people fated by climate to be barbarians? Perhaps, if only that Aristotle considers Greek peoples to display the same range of dispositions internally – European,

Asiatic and Greek. So there has to be something additional to geographical location that makes a people barbaric. Actually, Aristotle rarely uses the term "barbarian" except descriptively. He is far more interested in examining the analytical difference between "ethnos," which he characterizes as a group existing without a common purpose, and the "polis," a group who share a conception of the good life (Ward 2002). Aristotle defines the Persians as an ethnos: he does not believe that the despotic structure of empire allows for a deliberative, shared conception of the good.

Therefore, in Aristotle's conception, the difference between peoples is principally, albeit not solely, decided by their political regime. By this logic, there is nothing in nature that prevents Greeks from losing their civilization and becoming similarly barbarous. Pursuing the road to empire might lead to precisely such a loss.

But, once again, it's important to note that Aristotle's defense of the polis against imperial degeneration is at the same time a defense of the model colony-city – a small, autonomous, and hierarchical society. This conservative defense not only requires Aristotle to make a distinction between slave, barbarian, and citizen, regardless of which peoples might populate such distinctions at any time. It also requires a defense of the patriarchal household that provides the opportunity for male heads of those households to be citizens.

Once more, let's be careful with our reading of Aristotle. He does not claim that males represent the apex of the species, nor that the essence of humanity lies in sex differentiation (see Henry 2007). But he does identify the primary difference of sex in terms of the ability to produce semen. When it comes to species reproduction, females provide only the inert matter, while males sculpt the form. Shaping and changing human nature – that's a man thing. When that shaping occurs through politics, as is the nature of humans – this too is a man thing.

In modeling the small self-determining colony-city, Aristotle presumes that the nature of politics is best served by patriarchal hierarchy, although not imperialism. But is a hierarchical polis the only regime through which humans can deliberate in order to attain and preserve the good life? Put another way, has nothing of value for the good life ever been thought of or said by those who exist at the bottom of or outside of that hierarchy: metics, women, slaves, and barbarians?

This is the kind of question that I'll be returning to in every chapter and especially in the book's conclusion. For now, it's important to realize that such a question would be outside the logic of Aristotle's critical conversation with Athenians. Slaves have no capability to collective deliberate, barbarians, no culture through which to do so, and women no semen. By this reasoning, who would ever presume that these lesser subjects could conceptualize the good life differently – perhaps even more reasonably and justly? Which leads to another question: what goes un-thought of due to Aristotle's constraining logic?

There exists a strong possibility that Aristotle's discussion of the natural slave is directed against a social movement that, shortly before his time, regarded slavery as an affront to natural law. An influential rhetorician called Alcidamas had claimed that "the divinity ... left everyone free, nature made no one a slave" (Cambiano 1987, 31). This claim still resonated across Aristotle's political landscape. How large was this anti-slavery movement? Who comprised it? What did slaves think of it, and did they contribute intellectually to a conception of the polis that did not accept the moral worth of patriarchal hierarchy, as Aristotle did? Might their thoughts and actions have resonated so much in Aristotle's age that he felt they required a response (see Burns 2003)?

It is difficult to reconstruct in any detail the anti-slavery movement in fifth-century Athens. Perhaps ancient Greece is too far away. But our own colonial and imperial legacies are not. 1492, the year in which Columbus began the imperial conquest of what we now call the Americas, is as close to us as the Roman building of Hadrian's Wall is to Aristotle's birth. The time between our current decade and the formal end of most European empires is actually less than the span of Aristotle's lifetime. Expanding our geographical and historical vistas to match an inquiring imagination helps us to think politics anew.

For instance, it is not only possible to trace a tradition of black abolitionism in the Americas; we can also reconstruct African conceptions of the good life predicated upon the outlawing of slavery. In 1965, Youssouf Tata Cissé transcribed an Oath of the Mande Hunters that had been orally recounted since 1222 in the region of West Africa now encompassed by Mali (Nesbitt 2014, 11). The Oath arose at a moment of great flux in the region. Expanding empires brought war, and war brought captives that became slaves. Slave trading in West Africa was connected to global trading routes from the 620s onwards.

In response to this turmoil, the Oath of the Mande Hunters declares that "every human life is a life," and that "no one life is superior to any other" (Neocosmos 2014). The Oath defines a human being in some detail as a corporeal body that requires subsistence and which is also animated by an independent spirit. This independence of body and spirit affirms specific rights of the human to dispose of her own person as she sees fit, to act in the way she wishes, and to utilize the fruit of her labor as she decides. For these reasons, the Oath asserts that both hunger and enslavement must be banned. While the Oath is supposed to apply to Mande peoples in particular, it is proclaimed "for the ears of the whole world."

The Oath is best understood as part of a shifting tradition of inquiry into fundamental conceptions of human nature and politics. It is enunciated in an intentionally universal register, one that matches that of Alcidamas: all humans have equally valuable and valid lives. Furthermore, the rights the Oath affirms are "negative" in the sense that no one can take away a human's independence, as well as "positive" in the sense that resources must be distributed among humans. In these ways, the Oath of the Hunters provides a conception of the good life that, unlike Aristotle's, cannot abide slavery and must be based upon an equitable satiation of human needs and human spirit beyond household hierarchies.

The Oath is said to appear three hundred years before the beginning of the so-called Atlantic "slave trade," and over five hundred and fifty years before the American Declaration of Independence and the French Declaration of the Rights of Man and the Citizen. Neither Declaration, as celebrated as they are, matched the radical universality and equity of the Oath, although the revolutionary constitution of Hayti in 1805 certainly did. Remember that the Oath is orally recounted in various forms across this time span. It does not simply disappear, although it is not heard by all. Nowadays you might hear it in the proclamation that Black Lives Matter. Who, then, invented the idea of human freedom?

In our own time, some scholars have claimed that decolonizing the study of politics can only be a vulgar act of racial silencing, i.e. a muting of white European men just because they are white, European and men. I would hope you might now agree that decolonizing politics presents a far deeper challenge to us all: how expansive do we dare to make our conversation about politics? How deeply do we wish to critique what is presented to us as convention? How democratic do we wish our study of politics to be?

Organization of the Book

In making Aristotle uncanny, I've introduced you to some key maneuvers that we will be making in each chapter of the book as we seek to decolonize the study of politics, that is, the discipline of political science. Let me clarify these moves for you.

Firstly, in each chapter we will recontextualize political thinkers within the imperial and colonial contexts that form the backdrop to their ruminations. For instance, Aristotle is writing from within an imperial epoch where not one but two imperial powers are encroaching upon Athenians. Moreover, settler colonialism has created the very polities in which Aristotle teaches and that he moves between. Many textbooks present Aristotle as the philosopher of the good life – the examiner of the citizen in the polis. But that vision would only reveal to you half of the story. Aristotle examines a polis under threat from imperialism; and the independence he wishes to preserve for its citizens is one that is settler-colonial in its origin.

We are now starting to talk about the second maneuver. The act of recontextualizing thinkers by reference to imperialism and colonialism must make a difference to how we understand the logics of these thinkers' arguments. To put it pithily, recontextualization leads to reconceptualization. For example, instead of just presenting the citizen in and of himself, we have to understand citizenship by figuring out, as Aristotle actually did, the relationship of the citizen to the metic, the wife, the slave, and the barbarian. The citizen can no longer be considered a stand-alone category.

This means that reconceptualization is also an issue of epistemology – what counts as valid knowledge. Reconceptualizing especially involves tracking the connecting tissue that arranges concepts and categories in a logical fashion. For instance, Aristotle's hierarchies are not comprised of fixed objects in fixed positions. Instead, hierarchies are comprised of positions that can be occupied differently by different objects. The stakes at play in this reconceptualization must always be clarified by reference to empire and colonialism: for instance, Aristotle is trying to warn Athenian citizens that imperialism might force upon them the position of slaves.

So, decolonizing politics can't just be about retrieving histories of imperialism and colonialism. It must also be about finding concealed or ignored logics in popular and conventional arguments. And in the chapters that follow I will keep coming back to the way in which "colonial logics" animate concepts and categories in political science. Principally, you have to come out of this thing thinking differently. But that moves us to the third and most difficult maneuver: reimagining.

Let me introduce you to this maneuver by talking about "canons." The idea of a canon is at root a religious one, referring to a selection of scriptures considered to be true and sacred. When applied to academia, a canon refers to the set of authors and texts that are supposed to faithfully induct the student into the discipline. All disciplines have canons and political science is no exception. The so-called father of political science, Aristotle, often sits at the head of the canon.

But canons necessarily limit our understandings and imaginations. A critical evaluation of works within the canon – a task we have just undertaken with Aristotle – is necessary but not sufficient for the decolonizing mission. We must also try to glean the margins of power. We must imagine, at least in principle, that those who dwell in these marginalized positions have traditions of thought that are generally edifying. Why would we *not* imagine this to be the case, at least in principle?

That said, it's not always easy to find an author, a collective, or a movement that directly corresponds with or speaks back to the canon. The reason is simple but disturbing. Imperial centers talk to colonial margins but rarely listen back to them: that is broadly the case in academia as well as politics proper. And, because centers rarely listen back, you will not usually find colonial voices articulating themselves in the repositories and archives of politics, that is, the mainstream recorded history of politics.

Chinua Achebe, famous Nigerian novelist, once recanted an Igbo proverb when recalling why he became a writer: "until the lions have their own historians, the history of the hunt will always glorify the hunter" (Brooks 1994). Think for instance of the anti-slavery movement that Aristotle was writing against. There are hardly any records of it. What do I do, then: just let the slave masters tell the story? Pretend as if no slave has ever contested or had a thought about her slavery? No. I have to creatively seek out resonances, perhaps in unlikely places, and bring together the responses that I can find. The Mande Hunters can illuminate the issue of natural slavery, and they do not need to have read Aristotle to do so.

With this third maneuver we do not merely illustrate the ways in which some of the key arguments in political science have evolved with colonial logics and meanings. We also move those arguments into marginal locations – intellectually, conceptually, and/or empirically. We could even imagine that these marginal locations connect to each other, despite the wishes of the imperial center.

Thinking in this audacious manner allows us to place scholarly debates within broader constellations of logic and meaning. We gain a fuller understanding of the same issues. The master presumed he never had to know what the slave was thinking. After all, everyone told him that slaves couldn't think. But, in order to survive creatively, the slave had to know what she thought *and* how the master thought. Who would you turn to for an explanation of slavery: him or her? Put another way, studying only the center does not reveal to you the margins; but studying from the margins can inform you of the margins, the center, and their relationality; that is, the larger constellation of political activity (see Davis and Fido 1990).

Together, these three maneuvers are of what I take the project of decolonizing politics to consist. In what follows, I recontextualize, reconceptualize, and reimagine four popular subfields of political science: political theory, political behavior, comparative politics, and international relations. In each chapter I focus on a key theme associated with each subfield: universal rights in political theory, citizenship in political behavior, development in comparative politics, and war and peace in international relations. In the next section, I'll give you a short description of the aims of each chapter. But, before that, I want to make some general points about the aims and purposes of the book, as well as to come clean with at least one of its limitations.

It is absolutely *not* the case that all politics in the world have a colonial heritage or logic. This is not the claim of the book. But I do maintain that political science is formed as a discipline from imperial heritages and with abiding colonial logics. In short, the purpose of this book is to decolonize the *academic study* of politics, not politics per se. That said, you'll see by the end of the book that to pursue such a decolonization of knowledge requires us to commit to broader programs of global justice outside of the academy, narrowly conceived.

In pursuit of this decolonizing "impulse" I have selected various thinkers and themes not as true and full representations of every subfield: that would be impossible. Rather,

I've picked them because I think they bring the imperial heritages and colonial logics of the discipline into sharp relief; and I've selected their interlocutors from the margins in the way described above – imaginatively. In other words, don't read this book as if it is the authoritative account of political science. Read it to gain some practice in the art of decolonizing knowledge.

On this note, I want to justify to you the style of the book's prose. Often, social science is written in the third person – as an impersonal register of the outsider looking in. I'm hoping you'll have caught the problem with this register before you've even finished this sentence. Remember, we are involved in an uncanny enterprise. Uncanny enterprises require intimacy. You and I are taking this journey together.

Journeys are best represented as stories. Telling stories usually means, in some way, dwelling in the past. Most of the material that we'll work through is historical – from the fifteenth century up to the 1980s. But this is not a history book. We are using this material to recontextualize, reconceptualize, and reimagine the study of politics. I've picked stories that are heavily implicated in the formation of political science's subfields and which help to highlight the colonial logics that are integral to these formations. I've also picked stories that just as much bring to life different logics that contest these formations – in the academy and beyond. I'll provide some suggestions along the way, but it's going to be up to you to think about how all these stories resonate in the present. That's the "decolonizing" work that you'll have to do.

At this point you might be wondering if this book is a guide, a survey, or a series of provocations? Often, books that offer broad introductions into a field of study are presented in survey form, as non-committed and impartial engagements with various authors, issues, and arguments. I understand why. The writer does not want to tell you what to think but rather to guide you through the options. Once again, though, that strategy might not best fit a decolonizing agenda.

Stories always invoke some kind of travel – whether that be physical, intellectual, or ethical. We will be traveling from the center to the margins, from the imperial heartlands to the peripheral colonies, from the arenas of citizens to the spaces of migrants, from the offices of the powerful to the movements of the oppressed, and across physical, psychical, and social borders. Now, in order to journey, you have to commit somewhat to those whom you travel with, even if they annoy you. This commitment might sometimes mean taking their side, for a while at least. It's fine, by the way, to be critical of your traveling companions. I'm not trying to convert you or recruit you to anything. I'm simply suggesting: it's the journey that's critically instructive, not the destination.

Now for the limitations. I'm sure you'll find a number. But let me suggest one, right away. Most of the spaces that we will move in and through are Anglophone ones, that is, relics of Britain's 450-year empire: beginning with the plantations of Ireland in the 1550s and continuing to this day with the struggle over possession of Diego Garcia in the Indian Ocean. More than that, when we do venture into non-Anglophone territory (for instance, French Algeria), it is to engage with a thinker who is extremely well known in the English-speaking academy (i.e. Frantz Fanon). There is both a centering of English-speaking sources in the global academy, and beyond that, a centering of colonizer (European) languages. You should think about how we might need to decenter this colonial language preference in decolonizing work. That is Ngũgĩ wa Thiong'o famous message in *Decolonising the Mind* (1986).

Let me now sketch out for you the chapters that follow.

In chapter 2 we investigate the subfield of political theory. We focus on the question of what it means to be human, and how the capacity to reason is implicated in this question, especially as it pertains to the justification of rights. Political theory draws upon conversations that took place in the eras of the European Renaissance and subsequent Enlightenment. We consider how, in these eras, imperial expansion brought Europeans into contact with a diverse array of peoples, cultures, and practices. This diversity was tamed, if you like, by way of a fundamental philosophical distinction being made between properly human and not-properly human beings.

We engage specifically with the philosophical and anthropological writings of Immanuel Kant, and tease out the colonial logics of difference that accompanied his conception of the human. I'll be suggesting to you that the universal rights of which Kant boasts are only universal to those racially defined as properly human. We then grapple with the work of Sylvia Wynter, a Jamaican scholar of the humanities. Wynter is concerned with many of the same themes as Kant. But she arrives at a very different conclusion. Wynter seeks a conception of the human being that no longer rests upon the colonial and racist logic that distinguishes the properly human from the non-properly human.

In chapter 3 we turn to the subfield of political behavior. This subfield seeks to uncover how citizens engage with the political process and how that process responds to citizens. We begin our analysis in the late-nineteenth-century context of expanding empire and industrial urbanization in both Britain and the USA. In this era, scholars worried that the increasing movement and mixing of different peoples would negatively impact the quality of democracy. In response, they developed a race science that attributed the inheritance of degenerative abnormal behaviors to some races and the inheritance of progressive "normal" political behavior, conducive to an orderly democratic process, to the white Anglo-Saxon race. This science was informed by eugenics.

As part of this examination we look at the work of a set of scholars: Walter Bagehot, the British editor-in-chief of the *Economist* magazine, Woodrow Wilson, President of the United States, and John Watson, an American psychologist famous for coining the term "behaviorism." I'm going to make the argument that even if they refuted eugenics, all of these figures accepted the race logics of the science of heredity. We then explore a very different resolution to the division of citizenship into those who display normal versus abnormal political behavior. Frantz Fanon, a black clinical psychiatrist from Martinique, sought in his Algerian medical practice to repair the egos and psyches of those who had been made abnormal by structures of colonial rule. He envisaged a French citizenry that brooked no racial division on grounds of heredity.

In chapter 4 we address the subfield of comparative politics. We focus especially on the way in which comparativists have examined the distinctions between non-democratic and democratic societies and the varied paths of "political development" from one system to the other. Specifically, we track the colonial logic that inheres in what I will call the "paradox of comparison." This phrase references how difference might be accepted analytically, that is, as part of the way in which you understand human behavior, but disavowed "normatively," that is, as certain values and practices are set as the norm (the standard) by which all human groups should be evaluated and prepared for assimilation. We follow how scholars created and then re-shaped this paradox over a set of imperial eras from fifteenth-century Spanish colonization to twentieth-century decolonization.

Along the way, we look at the concept of "improvement" proffered by Adam Ferguson, a famous Scottish philosopher of the late eighteenth century; then we turn to the critique of "colonial development" made by famous anthropologist Bronislaw Malinowski in the early twentieth century; subsequently we examine the engagement by the US-based Committee on Comparative Politics with decolonization in the Cold War era. We then contrast the work of this Committee with that undertaken by a group of radical scholars who congregated at Dar es Salaam college, in Tanzania, in the late 1960s. I'm going to show you how Walter Rodney, Giovani Arrighi, and John Saul chose not to analyze developmental differences through a colonially induced paradox of comparison. Rather, they shifted their scope of analysis to the globally unequal relations of exploitation carved out by capitalist imperialism which delivered under-development to some and development to others.

In chapter 5 we scrutinize the subfield of International Relations (IR). Unlike most other subfields, IR displays a pronounced pessimism concerning the ability of humanity to enjoy the good life. In the absence of a world state, so the story goes, the logic of "anarchy" tends to lead to war and violence. Some scholars, however, call attention to globalization and the way in which its institutions of global governance mitigate conflict and provide some hope for the prospect of peace. We rethink this argument by retrieving the history of "good imperial governance" and its formative importance for the academic study of international politics. I'm going to make the argument that the pessimism evident in the study of IR is less a result of the logic of anarchy and more a colonial logic concerning the loss of empire.

In the course of this inquiry, we focus on Martin Wight, a very influential theorist of international politics. Wight is famous for introducing the concept of "international society" – a collective of diplomats and statesmen who might mitigate the worst of anarchy and its violent and warlike tendencies. I'm going to show you that Wight based his idea of international society on the British Commonwealth model of good imperial governance, while he increasingly associated the worst elements of anarchy – war and violence – with anti-colonial self-determination. Then we turn our attention to the Nuclear-Free and Independent Pacific movement of the late twentieth century. Led by Pacific women, this peace movement confronted nuclear war, military imperialism, and settler-colonialism as intersecting axes of oppression. I'm going to suggest that peace movements in the service of anti-colonial self-determination provide us with a very different insight into the causes and prospects for peace on a global level.

In the conclusion to the book, we return to Aristotle. Having identified the key colonial logics implicated in the subfields of political science we consider the extent to which Aristotle's critique of politics can be utilized as a resource for confronting these logics and decolonizing the study of politics. I'm going to argue that while Aristotle was anti-imperial, he nonetheless wished to preserve the patriarchal hierarchies that placed the citizen at the center of the political world and which moved others to the margins. We then put Aristotle in conversation with Gloria Evangelina Anzaldúa (1942–2004), a Chicanx queer theorist, who presents the craft of "border thinking." With Anzaldúa we evaluate the possibilities of studying politics from the margins with an intention to erase the power hierarchies that consistently recreate centers-with-citizens and marginal-peoples-on-borders.

–2–
Political Theory

In my experience, whenever a student hears the word "theory" they freeze. It's understandable. Theory is an amorphous word: it seems to imply everything yet references nothing of substance. Aristotle never clearly defines what he means by theory. But it does seem to involve something to do with our human nature.

Recall that for Aristotle nature is neither what is accidental nor necessary but something stable enough to be studied and variable enough to make any such study imperfect. Remember, too, that Aristotle defined the nature of human being in political terms as a collective deliberation toward choosing the best course of action to attain the good life. Given the fact that the study of nature would always be imperfect, the study of politics would always have to be a deliberative discussion about what might be best for any polity within a particular time and space.

Starting with Aristotle, we could say that theorizing implies some kind of self-reflection on our human nature. Self-reflection of this sort requires perspective and context, a situating of what appears familiar against an unfamiliar backdrop in time and space. Moreover, as Roxanne Euben (2004) points out, "theoria" in both classical Greek and Islamic philosophy can also infer travel – a dislocation from one context to another which allows a new perspective on the human condition. Interestingly, this association between theorizing and traveling is evident in much of the written material that makes up the corpus of political theory.

As a subfield of political science, political theory draws most of its key authors from Europe's Renaissance (15th–16th centuries) and Age of Enlightenment (17th–19th centuries). It's in the Renaissance, so the story goes, that self-reflection on the human condition was recovered from ancient civilizations after an age of medieval religious dogma. This study on the human condition was called "humanitas" – nowadays we call it the "humanities." The Enlightenment then turned this critical reflection into a projection of humanity's potential to evolve past all existing social and natural limitations. Crucially, both Renaissance and Enlightenment scholars were fascinated by reports of missionaries, traders, and adventurers of the Mediterranean, of the diverse and strange lands and peoples to its east and south, as well as the newly "discovered" Americas.

But here's the thing. On the one hand, these travelogues helped to clarify for European philosophers what the potential of humanity was to enjoy the "good life," what rights would realize this potential, and what governing arrangements might support such rights. On the other hand, these travelogues gave rise to a sense that this potential could only be achieved by Europeans due to their superior ability to reason upon the human condition. Paradoxically, political theory was all about the human experience (catalogued via travelogues) and, at the same time, all about a particular subset of humanity (the Europeans who wrote and read these travelogues).

Political theory is usually taught as an extended conversation with past and present thinkers. By and large, the focus rests on what past thinkers have said about the arrangements that guarantee the "good life." In this respect, the extent, adequacy and origin of rights are especially important to political theory. Fewer conversations have been had on what past thinkers said about what constitutes the "human." Far fewer conversations have been had over the degree to which this constitution had a colonial logic that distinguished properly human groups from not-properly human groups. Well, that's what we are going to focus on in this chapter.

In the first part, I am going to recontextualize those traditions with which political theorists begin their conversation on humanity, reason, and rights. I'm going to argue that Renaissance scholarship made a distinction between those properly human beings whose religion-based civilization enabled human potential – Catholic (and later Protestant) Christians – and those whose religion disabled such potential – Jews, Muslims, and heathens. I will engage with a very influential Enlightenment philosopher, Immanuel Kant (1724–1804), who sought to task the humanitas project to address the relationship between rights and reason.

Kant is famous for proposing that humans share the same ability to reason about their existence, and that this ability can be used to provide a universally applicable set of rights by which humans can live together in equality. I'm going to reconceptualize Kant's philosophy of rights. Specifically, I'm going to bring these writings of Kant into conversation with another set of his writings on anthropology – the study of diverse human conditions.

I will show how, in his anthropological writings, Kant maps out a particular geography of race which betrays a fundamental logic of difference: the white race can fulfill human potential; the other races cannot. I will then suggest that the universal rights of which Kant boasts are only universal to those racially counted as properly human, that is, white European men. When it comes to the rest of humanity, Kant provides a practical guide for their colonization.

In the second part, I will reimagine these issues by positioning Sylvia Wynter (1928–) in counterpoint to Kant. A Jamaican scholar of the humanities, Wynter is concerned with many of the same themes as Kant. But she arrives at a very different conclusion as to what reason does and what we might need to do with our reason to reach our human potential. In fact, Wynter wants to revolutionize the humanitas so that it no longer rests upon the colonial and racist logic that distinguishes the properly human from the non-properly human.

Wynter identifies the genesis of this distinction with lay scholars of the sixteenth-century Spanish empire, who recast the image of humanity in the form of a Christian rational man. In contrast, indigenous peoples of the Americas and enslaved Africans were cast as irrational and not-properly human. By the nineteenth century, Wynter argues, the image of humanity became a biological one, wherein white heredity determined whether one was properly human or not.

With the help of neurobiology, Wynter documents how quintessentially human it is for our mind-body to cast our sense of self as part of a collective that is properly human versus other collectives who are not. Yet Wynter also points out that those who have experienced the racist margins of being human might craft a route by which we can embrace a pluralistic image of humanity, wherein all are equally human. Through critical self-reflection Wynter suggests that we can set aside the colonial and racist logic of dividing humanity into the properly and not-properly human. This opens up the opportunity for us to change the very nature of our humanity.

Kant: Humanitas and the Anthropos

The Italian poet Francesco Petrarca (1304–1374) is believed to have first retrieved the ancient Roman pursuit of Humanitas for European Christendom scholarship. In 1333, Petrarca found a manuscript of the Roman statesman Cicero, which advocated the study of rhetoric, poetry, history, and moral philosophy for an education considered befitting a cultivated man. Humanitas was the kind of study that cultivated a civilized humanity. Study of this kind became the central dynamic of the Renaissance.

Such a dynamic begs the question: what counted as uncivilized? The Italian Renaissance was not an affair internal to the peninsula, but rather one that drew upon connections to the non-European world, in particular, the Islamic east. Much of the retrieval of the Greek and Roman classics in fourteenth to sixteenth-century Italy was made in conversation with Muslim traders and scholars, who shared the inland sea of the Mediterranean as much as Italians, Spanish, and French (Trivellato 2010). And yet, many of the scholars of the Italian Renaissance did not believe Muslims to be cultivated or civilized.

Consider ancient Cicero's advice to his brother: "if fate had given you authority over Africans or Spaniards or Gauls, wild and barbarous nations, you would still owe it to your Humanitas to be concerned about their comforts, their needs, and their safety." Here, Cicero seems to have depended upon Aristotle's distinction that we encountered in the last chapter between "ethnos" – a group existing without a common purpose – and the "polis" – a group who share a conception of the good life. That is, the civilized were able to conceive of and deliberate collectively on the good life; the uncivilized could not conceive of or work toward the good life.

Cicero's advice therefore pivoted on a distinction between those groups able to use their reason to pursue human potential and those that could not do so. This distinction resonated across the centuries into Petrarca's times, but there took on a religious gloss. It was, after all, an era defined by European Christendom's crusades into the Holy Lands of the Bible. Petrarca himself was alarmed at the expansion of the Ottoman empire westward across Anatolia and the Balkans toward Catholicism's heartlands.

For Petrarca, then, Humanitas inferred a religious kind of crusading education. Not only did a person's character have to be refined along moral, cultural, and aesthetic lines; just as importantly, the Christian nature of that character had to be proselytized across the world to counter the insurgence of heathens. The pursuit of Humanitas was "apocalyptic" in the Christian sense, meaning, a "final revelation." Only Christian civilization could unveil or reveal the end-state of humanity on earth, regardless of the fact that Muslim scholars had made major contributions to the retrieval of the classical heritage (Bisaha 2001).

By the Age of Enlightenment, another term came to represent human potential. Originally, the Greek word "anthropos" was used by first-century CE gnostics (Jewish and Christian seekers of spiritual knowledge) to reference Jesus Christ, the Son of God who lived and died a human life. In short, anthropos referenced the sacredness of being human. But you'll probably be more familiar with the term anthropology, which combines anthropos *and* logia (study) so as to refer to the study of human being. Interestingly, the Gnostics never connected "logia" to "anthropos." That kind of study only arose much later, in Renaissance France.

Straddling the French Renaissance and Enlightenment eras stood Comte de Buffon (1707–1788), who was especially influential in popularizing anthropology as a form of study. He is known primarily for his contributions to natural history. Influenced by all the new "discoveries" of species and humans made with the European colonization of the Americas, Buffon wrote a pivotal essay in 1749 on physical anthropology.

In *Of the Varieties of the Human Species* Buffon made the case for "monogenism" – the idea that all races of humanity derive from a single origin. He also argued that the original human represented by Adam and Eve was Caucasian, and that succeeding racial diversity could be accounted for in terms of the "degenerative" effects of humanity's spread across the world. Buffon's essay is important because it shifted the meaning of anthropos considerably. No longer referencing humanity as a sacred state to be aspired to, Buffon presented a de-sacralized object to be studied. Additionally, this new study of the human referenced a diversity of conditions, where an original type has degenerated into different races.

In sum, Humanitas was a kind of study that proposed a hierarchical division between those who could cultivate a civilized humanity and those who could not. Anthropology was a study that similarly divided humanity, this time into non-degenerate humans who could actualize the potential of their species – revealing/making the good life on earth – and degenerated humans who could not. The question then arises: what consequence did this division of humanity have on the corpus of political theory?

Let's now turn to one of the most influential Enlightenment theorists: Immanuel Kant. Like many German scholars in the latter eighteenth century, Kant pursued the idea of enlightenment (*Aufklärung*) as part of the Humanitas project: education had to cultivate the youth so that they could become civilized and help fulfill human potential. However, Kant became convinced that such a task required a radical rethinking of what the human faculty of reason was and how it could be applied to the real world in the form of rights.

Kant was famous for arguing that it was not God or nature that gives us our humanity but the faculty of reason itself. It is no exaggeration to say that Kant was obsessed with reason. In his estimation, reason was "architectonic" – a bringing together of various human experiences into an organized whole. What's more, Kant considered this "whole" to be "a priori" to experience, meaning, that all humans already carried in their minds certain categories that rendered experience knowable. For example, Kant would probably say that the absence, presence, or diffraction of light is only ever experienced by humans through the category of "color." Particular colors come to neatly stand in for the messy and unspeakable reality of diffracted and diffused photons. In short, we don't experience photons; we experience the category of colors.

Experience could never be known in-and-of-itself, argued Kant; rather, all that could be known with certainty were the categories that the mind used to make sense of that experience. There was, then, an unavoidable gap between the-world-as-it-is and the world-as-I-understand-it-to-be. The world-as-it-is was uneven, imperfect, differentiated (comprised of difference), particular. The categories of the mind, the-world-as-I-understand-it-to-be, were perfect, pure, and universal.

This gap between reality and reason took on huge importance to Kant when he considered how humans should co-exist in an imperfect world and how this co-existence required certain rights to be upheld universally across all individuals. For this worldly task, Kant divided the act of reasoning into two kinds. "Pure" reflection on the human experience was all about inquiring into the "a-priori" categories that made up the whole of understanding. Alternatively, "practical" reason was a reflection on how pure understandings should be applied to an imperfect world.

To this end, Kant (1991b, 133) provided "practical reason" with a "categorical imperative," meaning, a dictate that all individuals *should* follow, regardless of how the world *really* was. "Every action," claimed Kant (1991b, 133), "which by itself or by its maxim enables the freedom of each individual's will to co-exist with the freedom of everyone else in accordance with a universal law is *right*." Put another way: do unto others as you would have done unto yourself. It's no exaggeration to say that this maxim is foundational to any articulation of what we nowadays call universal rights.

How might an individual learn about the imperfections of the world in order to be equipped to make reasoned judgments upon it? To assist reason in calibrating toward an imperfect and unknowable world, Kant turned to anthropology. Hence, we will now connect his meditations on reason to his exploration of human diversity.

Anthropologists usually travel. At first glance, it might appear that Kant had very little travel experience to draw upon. He is famous for being very provincial, rarely journeying far from his home town. But this does not mean that Kant did not have an interest in the wider world. Presently his home town is in Russia and called Kaliningrad. But in his own time, it was called Königsberg and was the capital of East Prussia, as well as a major seaport for international trade. Kant's best friend was a worldly British merchant called Joseph Green, and Kant shared a long friendship with Green's business partner, Robert Motherby.

Kant was extremely curious about human geography in a world increasingly interconnected through imperial trade networks. Do you remember that the word "theoria" can infer travel, and that traveling was considered a good way to sharpen self-reflection? Well, if Kant rarely traveled, he did undertake many a vicarious journey through texts. Kant read European travelogues voraciously, most of which were published in his own lifetime. In footnotes to his philosophical treatises we come across, for example, James Cook's *Journals* of his Pacific voyages, Jean-Baptiste Demanet's *New History of Africa*, Fredrik Hasselquist's *Voyages and Travels in the Levant*, and Jonas Hanway's *Remarkable Occurrences* covering travels in Russia and Persia.

Travelogues assisted Kant in examining how the faculty of reason might be universally shared among humanity. But, as his examinations proceeded, he became increasingly interested in the ways in which human predispositions and characteristics had been modified to better suit various locales. This interest is evident in one of Kant's earliest attempts to make practical sense of the empirical diversity of human experience in an essay entitled *Observations on the Feeling of the Beautiful and Sublime* (1764).

In this text, Kant divided the ability to receive and feel experiences into two categories: the beautiful and sublime. Beauty referenced the aesthetic sense, the capability to be moved by feeling; the sublime referenced a noble form of virtue. Kant believed that having the capability to be moved by the sublime made one superior to those who were moved only by beauty. Humans differed quite significantly in these capabilities. While Kant accepted that, in principle, men and women could feel both the beautiful and sublime, he noted that women tended to gravitate to the former and men to the latter. In other words, men had more of a natural ability to plumb the depths of human experience than women. Similarly, Kant claimed that although all European peoples experienced both the beautiful and sublime, some nations felt one more than the other.

Kant then extended his geographical map further afield, and here the differences between peoples' capabilities to feel became far starker. Kant found the Indians and Chinese to be capable only of grotesque feelings; the indigenous peoples of America mostly lacked feeling; and "negroes" had "by nature no feeling rising above the ridiculous" (Kant 2010, 50–61). Kant drove this last point home by referencing the travelogue of Jean-Baptiste Labat, a visitor to the French islands of the Caribbean:

Father Labat reports that a negro carpenter, whom he
reproached for haughty treatment of his wives replied:
you whites are real fools, for first you concede so
much to your wives, and then you complain when they
drive you crazy. There might be something here worth
considering, except for the fact that this scoundrel was
completely black from head to foot, a distinct proof
that what he said was stupid. (Kant 2010, 61)

This quote has been used many times as proof of Kant's
racism. For this reason, it's worth noting that Kant badly
misrepresented Father Labat's observations. Here is what the
Father actually reported, in the text that Kant referenced:

I often enjoyed seeing a negro carpenter from our house
of Guadeloupe when he dined. His wife and children
were around him, and served him with as much respect
as the best-educated servants serving their master; and
whether it was a holiday or Sunday, his sons-in-law
and his daughters did not fail to be there, and to bring
him some little presents. They made a circle around
him, and entertained him while he was eating. When
he had finished, his pipe was brought to him, and then
he would tell them to go eat with the others. They gave
him due reverence, and moved to another room, where
they went to eat together with their mother.
    I sometimes reproached him for his gravity, and gave
him the example of the governor who ate every day
with his wife; to which he replied that the governor
was no wiser; that he well believed that the whites had
their reasons, but that they too had theirs; and that, if
we were concerned with how white women were proud
and disobedient to their husbands, it would be clear
that the blacks, who always hold them in respect and
submission, were wiser; and more than the whites on
this matter. (Labat 1724, 2: 54 my translation)

Contrasting the original text and Kant's interpretation, it
becomes clear that the carpenter was no "scoundrel" in

Labat's eyes as he was for Kant, but rather a respected patriarch. Moreover, Labat admitted that this "negro" was able to argue convincingly that he was a better patriarch than the white man. But Kant could not accept this point because it would undermine his own claim that European men were best at turning their human experience into noble virtue (see Shell 2001). That's why Kant was compelled to misrepresent Labat's evaluation by dismissing the carpenter's opinion on account of the fact that skin color determined the ability of the human to exercise reason.

Kant really was as obsessed with race as he was with reason! And as he radically rethought the nature of reason, Kant tightened the fit between skin color and the capacity to exercise one's full humanity (see Eze 1995; Robert Bernasconi 2001). Kant made this fit ever tighter over the course of a decade's work. He began to turn the screw in 1775, in an essay entitled *Of the Different Races of Human Beings*.

In this text, Kant (2011b, 84) drew upon Buffon's work, thus introducing the French study of anthropology to the German academy. Kant was especially interested in Buffon's proposition that animals who produced fertile offspring together must belong to the same physical species. Kant also accepted (as we shall see) Buffon's speculation that humans would degenerate as they spread across the earth.

However, Kant departed from Buffon's belief that the resulting differentiation of the species was accidental. Rather, Kant conceived of this differentiation as part of nature's master-plan. Nature had placed in humans "hidden provisions for all kinds of future circumstances," especially the ability to live in "all climates and ... every [type of] soil." Air and sun combined, Kant (2011b, 88) argued, to generate certain "germs" that then established a sub-species of the human. Given this logic, the creation of sub-species had to be understood as part of the natural plan for humanity to disperse, populate, and rule the earth.

But what counts as a sub-species? Kant explained that when different sub-species procreated together they produced "half-breeds." Ok, but how do you know a half-breed when you see one? Because, proclaimed Kant, the color of the child would be different from each of the parents. Not so much the hair color, to be clear: blond and brunettes were not sub-species. Rather, it was all about – you guessed it – skin. Kant (2011b, 85–87) speculated that there were four sub-species of humanity – white, negro, hunnish, hindu – each of which was categorized by reference to skin color and climate – high blonds (of humid cold), blacks (of humid heat), copper-reds (of dry cold), olive-yellows (of dry heat).

Now, think back to Kant's comments on Father Labat's carpenter. Color, for Kant, intonated not just different aesthetics, but different predispositions and cultural character. Put another way, skin color became an index to the geographical map of uneven human capacities. The "negro," again, demonstrated these differences most clearly for Kant:

> The negro, who is well suited to his climate, namely, strong, fleshy, supple, but who, given the abundant provision of his mother land, is lazy, soft and trifling. (Kant 2011b, 93)

Was humanity always degenerated by climate? Luckily, answered Kant (2011b, 94), the climate that "birthed" whites was "rightly taken for that region of the earth in which the most fortunate mixture of the influences of the colder and hotter regions are found." Shifting Aristotle's identification of the perfect climate from the Mediterranean to Europe in general, Kant asserted that whites possessed "the perfect mixture of the fluids and the strength" of humanity. Indeed, whites were the closest among all sub-species to the human "phylum" – a term that for Kant indicated an origin point that birthed the species itself. Whites were the least degenerated, while all other sub-species degenerated irreversibly from whiteness.

While *Of the Different Races of Human Beings* introduced anthropology to the German academy, Kant's next text on the subject explicitly introduced the concept of race (*rasse*). In *Determination of the Concept of a Human Race* (1785), Kant dismissed empirically driven inquiries into natural history for their inability to clarify the purpose of nature when it came to humanity. In effect, Kant was criticizing his own previous work. Instead of arguing that the differentiation of humanity into colored sub-species was a natural occurrence, Kant (2011a) now proposed something even more extreme: race was not a natural phenomenon but a category of the mind. This was a subtle yet significant shift in Kant's argument. After a number of philosophical trials, Kant finally made race something that existed prior to experience (see especially Larrimore 2008).

We can tease out the consequences of this shift by turning to one last text that Kant subsequently wrote: *Conjectures on the Beginning of Human History* (1786). I'm going to give a generous reading of this narrative first of all. Reason, Kant opined, created "free choice" so as to bring "man" out of the "state of servitude" that accompanied the "rule of instinct." Reason won over animal impulses, especially in terms of cultivating the ability to delay gratification, which then progressively enabled a sense of decency and "true sociability" (Kant 1991a, 224). With this accomplished, reason provided for humans an anticipation of the future and the idea of living through one's offspring. Ultimately, this led man to realize that "he is the true end of nature" and that, as such, he must treat all other individuals as an end in themselves, rather than use them as a means toward his own ends.

What a wonderful story of universal rights: nature directs that each individual must be treated the same, regardless. I guess if you never read Kant's anthropological texts you'd think that this really was such a story. But let's place this prescription next to Kant's writings about differences between humans, that is, his anthropology of racial difference.

For this alternative reading, we need to recollect a few points. For Kant it was reason that made humanity meaningful, not God or nature. Recall also that for Kant it was not possible to provide a factual history of the world-as-it-is. Instead, the purpose of narration was conjectural: a story did not provide facts, i.e. claims-about-how-the-world-really is, but regulative guidelines, i.e.

this-story-tells-you-what-we-should-do-in-the-world. Finally, note that Kant now considered race to be a universal category of the mind by which humans made sense of real-world differences in the pursuit of judgment as to what course of actions to rightfully pursue.

A second pass at Kant's story of human progress reveals it to be a particular story of white men treating each other as ends rather than means. Here's Kant's conjectural story of human/racial evolution. The outside of Europe is populated by various races whose character and dispositions are degenerated by their geographical climate. They cannot exercise reason sufficiently. Hence, they cannot fulfill nature's design. And no amount of race-mixing can mitigate the sub-human standard of these races. Only the white race can traverse the earth without fear of degeneration, because only the present-day white race has inherited and retained all the germs necessary to pursue reason – humanity's grand design. Pragmatically speaking, Kant's use of reason is not for the pursuit of universal rights but rather, universal rights for whites, and racist, colonial occupation for others.

Japanese philosopher Osamu Nishitani (2006) helps to clarify the stakes at play in the reconceptualization of reason and rights that we've just worked through. He argues that enlightenment thought is shot through with a fundamental distinction between humans who are endowed with the reason to pursue Humanitas (education to cultivate human potential), and the anthropos (varieties of "non-Western human") who are not equipped to actualize human potential. The pursuit of Humanitas is designed to make a racially delineated "us" better humans; the study of the anthropos, i.e. anthropology, is designed to help "us" govern a racially delineated "them" more effectively. In the history of enlightenment thought, this pursuit and this study proceed simultaneously.

Many theorists are embarrassed by the treatises on race written by so many luminaries of universal rights. I entirely understand why some would prefer to leave those texts untaught on the library shelves, there to gather dust. But this doesn't erase the fact that in belonging to the Humanitas project, political theory imbibes colonial logics. We should investigate the canon of political theory honestly. Because that investigation might tell us something about the way in which the very idea of the "human" is partial and discriminatory. And that might lead us to better assess the proclaimed universality of rights themselves.

Such an aspiration provokes a question: can we cultivate a conception of human potential (the Humanitas project) that brooks no distinction between the fully human and the not-properly human (anthropos)? To address this question requires some reimagining of the relationship between the human condition, reason and rights. For this, we're going to read Sylvia Wynter alongside and against Kant's philosophy. We'll see how Wynter engages with Kant's logical separation of the human and the not-properly human, yet arrives at a stunningly different explanation and prognosis of this separation for the realization of human potential.

Wynter: Man1 and Man2

Wynter (2015, 202) self-identifies as a "Western [or] westernized" academic working in the "human sciences." But she also writes as an intellectual whose trajectory has been profoundly shaped by her Caribbean heritage. Location means something. The world comes to Kant in good part through the trading port of Königsberg. For Wynter, the anti-colonial uprisings in the late 1930s Caribbean are foundational to her perspective on the world.

As her academic career takes shape in the 1960s, Wynter confronts the limits of Jamaica's post-independence intellectual life against the backdrop of the Rastafari and Black Power movements. Challenging the "white lie" that there is nothing to learn from the Caribbean experience, Wynter (1968, 24) presses her fellow Caribbean academics to accept a "black truth." The historical "uprootedness" that the Black Diaspora have experienced with slavery and its legacies should be understood as "the original model for the total twentieth-century disruption of man." With this claim, Wynter begins a project to revolutionize the humanities.

At the start of this chapter we recontextualized the Humanitas project as part of a Christian fear of Islamic encroachment onto holy lands in the East. Now, we're going to lay on top of that a further recontextualization, this time pointing toward the West. (Some of Kant's references, for example to Father Labat, led us there too.) In fact, Wynter argues that the "discovery" of the Americas was largely responsible for transforming the newly retrieved study of Humanitas – and in fundamental ways.

In a similar fashion to Kant, Wynter's decades of working through the meaning of human experience also utilizes European travelogues. But while Kant used these texts to racialize the fully rational human being as white, Wynter uses these texts to address the question "What is human?" from the perspective of the anthropos – those racialized as non-rational and not-properly human. Top of Wynter's list of writers is Christopher Columbus.

Wynter accords great importance to the year that Columbus chanced upon the island of Guanahani (San Salvador in the present-day Bahamas). Prior to 1492, she points out, the human experience was defined by Christian theologians in terms of a clash between the "spirit" and "fallen flesh" (Wynter 2003, 278). This clash was then projected onto a map of the cosmos: the heavens being the realm of spiritual perfection; the earth being the realm of "fallen" man. Additionally, the temperate regions of Earth – with Jerusalem at the center – were deemed to be held above the waters by God's grace. On these lands only could the fallen be redeemed. In contrast, the "torrid" regions of earth were uninhabitable, especially those lying past Cape Boujdour (presently in the Western Sahara, one of the world's last colonies, still largely controlled by Morocco).

For Wynter, Columbus's voyage was a notable event in so far as it challenged the sacred geography of Christendom. Christian theologians had previously assumed that "fallen man" could not know nature, because only God commanded it. Nonetheless, Marco Polo's adventures to the "Indies" had cracked open this presumption by positing a much wider distribution of humanity than was suggested by biblical lore and geography.

Wynter notices in the writings of Columbus an apocalyptic belief in the imminent second coming of Christ and the requirement for all humanity to be converted to the Christian faith. This belief, Wynter suggests, led Columbus to assert, heretically, that all the seas and oceans of the world must be navigable if the scattered flock of humanity were to be gathered in time for Christ's return (1991, 256). Columbus, influenced by Marco Polo's writings, suggested that a western passage to the Indies was actually possible. Just imagine the controversy when Columbus "found" land above the waters of the Caribbean Sea inhabited by peoples who were not catalogued in the Bible!

All this, Wynter suggests, led to the possibility that God might have created the earth, but he did not directly control it: humans did. How else could Taino – the indigenous peoples of the Caribbean – live in supposedly uninhabitable lands? This, though, inferred that humanity's potential was not directly dependent upon the grace of a deity but rather lay in the capacity of that deity's creation – humanity – to use reason to understand and utilize the laws of nature for themselves.

The focus on reason as key to unlocking human potential raised the prospect of a more reciprocal, egalitarian relationship between God and humanity. Wynter (2015, 190) notes that lay scholars of the Renaissance – those who did not officially work for the church – pioneered this shift. Henceforth, post-1492, the question that drove the Humanitas project was no longer addressed with a "theo-centric" answer – God decides (just think of Petrarca's hardcore Christianity) – but instead a "ratio-centric" answer – our reason determines. Or, as Wynter (2015, 190) puts it, the study of human potential was "de-godded."

Still, not everything new is brand new. Crucially, Wynter argues that these lay scholars carried over an older theological distinction between the salvaged (Christians) and those yet to be saved (the infidels and heathens). And this carry-over became one of the fundamental logics of colonial rule. In short, the hierarchy of God over man was levelled only to be replaced with a hierarchy of man over man.

To understand this re-imposition of hierarchy, Wynter leads us to examine the economy of Spain's global empire. In the centuries preceding Columbus's landfall, the Iberian Peninsula had been gradually taken back from the Moorish dynasties by Christian armies. (Moors were predominantly Muslims from North and West Africa.) In the process, land was expropriated from Moorish authorities and placed in the hands of their military conquerors. Some Muslim populations were even conscripted to bonded labor.

This system was subsequently exported to the Caribbean. Although the lands were "newly" discovered, Columbus categorized its indigenous peoples via the same distinctions that European Christendom had used to carve up the "old" world: Christians, infidels (Muslims and Jews) and heathens (non-Abrahamic so-called pagans). In the "new world," indigenous people were not considered enemies of the Christian faith like Muslims and other infidels, as they had yet to receive (let alone reject) the good news of the Gospel. They were therefore denoted as heathens. However, if indigenous peoples demonstrated no desire to convert to Christianity once they had received the good news, then they were treated as infidels and subject to the same conquest as Muslims and Jews.

By this logic, and through a very spurious legal process, indigenous land was taken by settlers, while indigenous populations were put into bonded labor, serving the agricultural or mining interests of the conquistadors. In 1519 indigenous peoples in present-day Puerto Rico were joined by the first enslaved peoples to arrive directly in the Americas from the African continent, specifically the coast of present-day Western Sahara. This economic system consolidated the Spanish state, as Wynter (1984, 30) puts it, into the "world's first global empire."

Wynter (1991, 266) argues that as lay scholars radically revised the study of humanity, they did so through the logics that served Spain's empire. The result was a "hybrid religio-secular" definition of the human as the Christian-rational Man. That is, to be Christian was to be rational which was to have dominion over the earth (on God's behalf). In distinction to this "Man" lay the infidels and heathens who populated the Atlantic economic system of extraction, expropriation and exploitation. Unlike Christian-rational Man "Indios" (indigenous peoples) were considered irrational and "Negros" (African peoples) to be the missing link between rational humanity and irrational animality.

Reflecting on this history of conquest, Wynter (2003) proposes that the Humanitas project was re-tasked to over-represent Christian-rational Man as the proper human in distinction to the not-properly human Indos and Negros. I know: the academic jargon here is daunting. But consider this. We can close our eyes and imagine the human in a multitude of ways: veiled, uniformed, naked, tattooed, dark-skinned, blue-eyed, hairy, bald, sitting, running, talking, writing, frowning, in unison with others, solitary, smelling of Frankincense, or of garlic etc. Now imagine that just one very specific type of human – a composite of particular images – comes to stand in for *the only true* image of humanity, for instance, a cross-wearing Christian man in European dressage who consistently proclaims his superior rationality. That's what Wynter means by over-representation. Other composite images can only be not-properly human to this properly human Christian-rational Man.

And that is Wynter's key point: the same intellectual movement that levelled the theological hierarchy between God (creator) and human (created) at the same time constructed just as fundamental a hierarchy *between* humans (properly and not-properly human). The Humanitas project carries an abiding paradox even into the Age of Enlightenment: the potential for human liberation through the use of reason comes with the oppression of most of humanity by a very particular type of human – the Christian-rational Man over-representing himself as the only true image of humanity.

Here's where the value of Wynter's work lies for the subfield of political theory. Wynter lays out the intellectual logic by which political theory becomes haunted – as Kant was – by the distinction between Humanitas (the educational project that over-represents humanity as Man) and the anthropos (the diverse range of not-properly human practices and cultures). In fact, it's amazing how neatly Wynter identifies the historical and philosophical heritage with which Kant crafts his anthropology.

Remember that, for Kant, reason and not God's grace is what makes us properly human. The white man, for Kant, is the purest human who possesses the seeds of all the potentialities of humanity, in distinction to the degenerate seeds scattered across the world which take root as not-properly human races. Only the white man can properly utilize his reason to navigate this world. The world is his. It's fairly clear that Kant's anthropology performs the same replacement of hierarchies that Wynter identifies in the Renaissance: from God over human to Man over-representing humanity.

Except that Kant does not present this Man in religious terms. Actually, we've just described Man1. But there is also a Man2. Wynter identifies this further shift in the image of Man as taking place around the nineteenth century, and linked to Britain's second imperial expansion into the Asian and African continents. In this new era, Man becomes an entirely secularized type and his religious roots vanish. Instead of Christianity and reason, it is biology and inheritance that make up the proper type of human. In a way, Kant's anthropology – full of phylums, seeds, races, and degenerative inheritances – pre-empts this further biological reimaging of humanity's potential.

We'll turn more fully to the question of racial heredity in the next chapter. For now, and in order to understand what Wynter is getting at with this shift from Man1 to Man2 we need to quickly unpack the notion of "phenotype." Usually when it comes to race we think about physical characteristics: skin-color, hair etc. True, the root of "pheno" in ancient Greek means "to show." Yet scientifically speaking, phenotype actually refers to all the observable characteristics of an organism, including behavior, not just looks. In racial phenotypes, the "look" is part of the "behavior" and vice versa. Just think about Kant's claim that the negro is stupid because he is black.

It might now not seem so strange that Wynter describes Man2 as *Homo oeconomicus*: an "economic man," who has evolved so as to be able to meet his needs and satisfy his interests through the capitalist market. Whiteness as a phenotype does not just mean pale skin, it also means a pale-skinned "bourgeois" man who pursues private property ownership and corporate interests. Man2's progeny is assured inheritance of the earth because only they can exploit nature and other humans in a way that will assure the accumulation of capital.

Concurrent with the rise of Man2, asserts Wynter, the not-properly human category or the idolater (Indos and Negros) is replaced with the colonial dark-skinned "native" who is associated with a vast reservoir of cheap and abused labor, the most stereotypical representation of which is the black African. This black/native does not have the competency to compete in the market: she is idle, far too communal, and imprudent; her progeny will be deselected by human evolution (Wynter 2003, 266).

Wynter suggests that the new over-representation of humanity by Man2 has led to the global crises that we currently face. With Man2, poverty, immiseration, and shortened lives can be explained away as a result of inherited biological incapacity to perform the actions necessary for survival – namely, to become economic man, amass property and accumulate capital just for yourself and your immediate family. If you take this as granted, then the inequalities that global capitalism creates cannot be morally repugnant because global capitalism is the mechanism through which humanity evolves and civilization triumphs.

Wynter warns that so long as Man2 is presumed to be the only proper human, rather than just a particular type of human being, then the global destruction authored in the name of this Man will continue. Take, for instance, global warming. That the climate crisis is termed "anthropogenic" is, for Wynter, a problem. This label infers that the crisis is caused by "generically human activities" rather than driven

by the particular interests of a particular subset of humans
– those who accumulate capital for themselves on a global
scale and don't give a damn about the environmental consequences (Wynter 2015, 232).

But Wynter is not satisfied with exposing the colonial over-
representation of Man as humanity. She wants to decolonize
the very study of our humanity – the Humanitas. She needs,
then, a theory of why it is that, when we conceive of our
shared humanity, we tend to keep reproducing hierarchical
differences between "us" – the properly human – and "them"
– the not-properly human. Wynter tackles this challenge
by canvasing a broad set of debates among philosophers,
sociologists, anthropologists, biologists, and neuroscientists
on the question of what makes the human condition specifically "human." Hold on tight, because things will now get
even more complex.

Wynter picks up on debates coming out of entomology (the
study of insects) concerning "eusociability" – a specific kind
of socializing undertaken to benefit a colony of organisms.
When rearing their young, colonies of animals and insects
cooperate due to their genetic similarity. But humans do not.
We, instead, have evolved a special and distinct capacity for
language. And words and meanings can create their own
processes of socialization – of cooperation – in excess of
genetic similarity.

Think, for example, of the varied meanings of the word
"family" in your own life, and who might be included or
excluded from that collective and for what specific reasons.
Are all these reasons strictly to do with genetic fit? Then
think also about how you might conceive of non-biological
relationships – close friends or colleagues – as also familial
relationships. Wynter's point is that humans practice a
distinct kind of eusociability – an "artificial" rather than
purely genetic one.

Given our distinctiveness, how might we think about the
human character of consciousness, as opposed to say, the
consciousness of insects or other animals? Recall that for Kant
human consciousness is "architectonic": our consciousness
is an organized system of categories that all humans carry

in their minds through which to understand experience. And remember that this "pure" reason, for Kant, must be practically applied, although only the white race can competently do so. In Kant's estimation, only the white race is equipped with the biology and rationality to travel the world and conquer it.

Wynter wants to demonstrate that, contrary to Kant, race is not a pre-existing category of the mind. For this task she draws upon neuroscience and the idea that each organism gains knowledge of their world predominantly via terms that enable them to seek an adaptive advantage. Put another way, each organism knows their world only through the process of seeking a reproductive benefit that will better suit them to their environment. No organism will primarily seek to know the world objectively but rather by evaluating their environment normatively in terms of "good" or "bad," that is, what is good or bad for the long-term reproduction of their species.

Let's now consider the analogy Wynter makes between the seeking of biological adaptive advantage and the seeking of social advantage. After all, humans must also know and classify the world in ways that might give an adaptive advantage to their sense of self. Wynter (1991, 262) expands on this claim by using one more analogy to biology.

"Autopoesis" refers to the self-maintaining chemistry of living cells, that is, the way in which they replicate themselves. By analogy, Wynter argues that human beings undertake subjective (rather than biological) autopoesis. Humans know their world in terms of what is deemed good or bad for the reproduction of their fictive collective. Basically, we know the world through the origin story that we give to our collective self – "us." From this origin story we determine what is good and bad for "us" – what has kept us going or has retarded our growth – in distinction to what is good or bad for the "others." That's our autopoesis: not genes and sperm, but the story we regularly tell ourselves about the fundaments of our humanity.

Perhaps you're convinced by Wynter's argument, perhaps not. But regardless, you might well feel a little unsettled that, in Wynter's conception, what makes the human condition

specifically human rests on analogy: an imagined correspondence between two very different elements – chemicals
and ideas. But in point of fact, Wynter makes a more
substantive connection between the stuff of natural science
(i.e. biology) and the stuff of human science (i.e. Humanitas).
She does so by turning to yet another science: neurobiology
– the biological study of the nervous system.

All living species, notes Wynter (2001), have a "natural
opioid system" that produces chemicals that signal reward
(you feel good for doing something that benefits your
organism) and punishment (you feel bad for doing the
opposite). Behaviors that seek adaptive advantage in the
organism's environment are regulated by the release of
these chemicals. For Wynter, when it comes to the human
condition, feeling good or bad is not genetically determined
but always mediated by a fictive eusociability. The stories
we tell about what is good for "us" in distinction to others
regulate and are regulated by chemicals.

Wynter (2001) draws out the significance of this neurosocial regulation of humanity by turning to the work of
a black psychiatrist from the French Caribbean island of
Martinique, Frantz Fanon. (We'll engage with Fanon in some
detail in the next chapter.) In his famous book *Black Skins
White Masks*, originally published in 1952, Fanon speaks of
how, when in Martinique, he did not believe himself to be
a *nègre* (black) but rather French. Descendants of slavery
in the French Caribbean told an origin story of themselves
as having been more civilized by their colonizers than their
savage African ancestors, the real "others" to their French
selves.

Now, while he was in the Caribbean, this collective sense
of self went unchallenged. But, when Fanon moved to France,
he was suddenly cast as the black "other" – a savage African
– to the French "we." Wynter explains Fanon's experience in
terms of autopoesis (collective self-making) and the neurosocial regulation of what is good for "us." The "truth" of the
Martiniquan is that it is not good for "us" to be black, but it
is good for "us" to be white, or at least, closer to white. But
when Fanon is in France, he is perceived by the French "us"

as black – not "us." He is forced to now know himself to be both a Man2 (French "bourgeois") but also as not-Man2 (just a "black").

How do you feel when your body is confronted with the "truth" that it is not properly human? Being described as a *nègre* in France, Fanon remembers suddenly feeling his whole sense of humanity slipping away and his body literally discombobulating. That's what chemical releases in the brain can do to you when the story of your humanity is refuted by those who have power to do so.

But Wynter then makes an important observation. Those of us who have never had our humanity challenged are far less likely to reflect on its deeply artificial nature, especially the way in which our neurobiology socially regulates the distinction between "us" as human and "them" as not-properly human. Alternatively, those of us whose lived experience is "liminal," who are on the edge of the "we" *and* the "them," might be able to attain a greater level of self-reflection, even despite the stories that the chemicals in their bodies tell. I guess this puts a different gloss on how theory is consonant with traveling. Those who are forced to travel across, between, alongside the "us"/"them" border might gain a faculty for self-reflection far greater than that of those who can remain comfortably at the center of the "us" story. We'll return to this possibility in the book's conclusion.

That said, it is possible to catch a bit of resonance between Wynter and Father Labat, who at least accorded to the carpenter from Guadeloupe (another French island neighboring Martinique) a capacity to reason about his and white people's humanity. Not so, of course, for Kant. In any case, shifting from Königsberg, the center of Kant's world, to the Caribbean margins, Wynter confirms her hunch, from all those decades ago in Jamaica, that the fate of humanity lay in the hands of the enslaved African and not the European master.

By shifting the "geography of reason" (Gordon 2005) in this way, Wynter straddles the dividing line in Kant's philosophy between pure and practical reason. Wynter is effectively saying that there is no such thing as "pure" reason

– a universally valid architecture through which to understand our experiences prior to our actually experiencing them. She is arguing that "practical" reason – normatively driven reasoning on our imperfect existence – is all there is. What Kant calls practical reason is better understood as autopoesis. Our judgments are already part of the origin story that crafts who "we" are and who "they" are not. These are no free floating "ideas," though. The story crafts, and is crafted by, our nervous systems.

By this reckoning, Wynter demolishes Kant's presumption that a certain race of humans is more biologically capable of utilizing their reason than other degenerative forms of human being. Wynter's argument reveals Kant's naivety. There is no higher truth to race beyond the origin story that Kant tells of his own "us" – the white race.

Wynter's shift in the geography of reason enables us to consider something quite audacious: "an entirely new answer to the question of who-we-are" over and against the presently destructive answer to be found in Man1 and then Man2. Wynter is after no less than a reinvention of Humanitas as the study not of the Man versus the anthropos but of a "universal human species," where to be the human "us" does not need to be predicated upon marking out a not-properly-human "other."

You might recollect that after having laid out his racist anthropology, Kant then conjectures on the beginning of human history, which is really a story of how Man over-represents humanity. Well, Wynter provides her own origin story of *Homo narrans*. The first cosmological event Wynter narrates as the origin of the physical universe; the second event is the origin of biological forms of life; and the third event arises out of Africa as humans take a different evolutionary route, increasing brain power so as to be able to manipulate symbols and language "in service of a unique capacity to tell stories" (Wynter 2015, 217).

To this chronology, Wynter adds one more prospective cosmological event, an intellectual one with as much consequence as the original Humanitas project post-1492. It is an event that might finally do away with the hierarchal and segregationist mode of defining the human, whether that be God over man, or properly humans over not-properly humans. It is the realization that our human condition is defined by our self-making through origin stories, and that this plurality of stories is precisely what is human about the human condition.

"*Homo*" is Latin for human being; "*sapiens*" is Latin for "discerning." *Homo sapiens* can be glossed as the "wise man." Wynter (2015, 194) introduces the premise of a new Humanitas project: "we are co-human" because we are *all* subject to the natural law that we narrate ourselves into being. Our potential is no longer defined by being *Homo sapiens* but by being "*Homo narrans.*"

Wynter's abiding provocation to us is this: if we are to be truly self-reflective of our human condition then we must realize that no one story can over-represent the human experience. No one has a right to define their humanity by rendering others as non-properly human. Through a new Humanitas of *Homo narrans*, we might be finally able to gather together our "collective human agency" to address the global challenges of the present – climate crisis, inequality, war etc. – caused by the over-representation of Man2 as the human (see Wynter 2015, 232).

Conclusion

Many of the debates in contemporary political theory focus on the extent, applicability and origins of rights. For instance, do you have rights by virtue of being human or due to the random fact that you were born in a particular country or to particular parents? As important as such debates are, they are inadequate if they do not address the colonial logics that constitute the "human" – a racialized man masquerading as humanity at large.

In this chapter, we've recontextualized the Humanitas project within a religious and imperial carving out of the distinctiveness and partiality of humanity. With this project, the Christian/rational/white man is the properly human being capable of realizing the species' potential, as opposed to the not-properly humans – the anthropos. We've reconceptualized the work of Immanuel Kant within this religious and imperial project. We've tracked how his philosophy of reason and rights accepted and reproduced the distinction between properly humans and not-properly humans. With Sylvia Wynter, we've reimagined the colonially induced and racialized logics that over-determine Man as humanity at large. We've even scoped out a new way of studying humanity's potential that does not seek to reproduce such distinctions.

To be fair, political theory has come a long way in addressing what makes humans human. Scholars such as Jane Bennett (2010) and Bill Connolly (2017) have made salient critiques of the fixed identities so often assumed in political theory. They have instead presented expansive visions of the relationship between humans and nonhuman forces, as well as on democracy as an intrinsically pluralistic affair. The question, I guess, is whether we can ever adequately expand and pluralize our conceptions of humans, non-humans, and rights, without having first decolonized the logics that presented us with the exclusionary "human being" in the first place (see Jackson 2018).

It's notable that the principal interlocutor of Wynter's work at present is most likely Katherine McKittrick (2015), a geographer and gender studies professor, not a political theorist (formally speaking). At a collective level, Wynter's work has been engaged with principally by those associated with the Caribbean Philosophical Association (CPA). Yet only a few of these scholars, for example, Jane Gordon (2014), Neil Roberts (2015) and Anthony Bogues (2010), are directly affiliated with the subfield of political theory.

Debates in the CPA revolve around a question: what does coloniality deem to be human? Coloniality – the persistence of colonial logics of thinking and doing even in the absence of formal colonial rule – is a term developed by the Modernity/Coloniality/Decoloniality (MCD) project. Largely associated with scholars and activists from Latin America such as Aníbal Quijano, Enrique Dussel, and Walter Mignolo, the

MCD project makes its departure point the colonization of the Americas rather than the European Enlightenment (see in general Escobar 2007, Mignolo and Walsh 2018). The project further examines how settler colonialism and plantation economies make some humans human and other humans less-than-human. Some associated scholars, such as Silvia Rivera Cusicanqui (2015), work with the marginalized knowledge traditions of indigenous peoples.

Might these conversations be of utility to the subfield of political theory? Surely, they are of direct relevance to debates concerning what rights might come after the "human" and what kinds of arrangements for the good life might follow. Perhaps it would be worth looking back to 1492 as we seek an orientation forward. And for new insights perhaps we should consult the sages on the margins – in Jamaica, Martinique etc. – instead of those who live their whole life in the centers, and comfortably in their own skins.

In the next chapter we will move to consider a different question that arises out of the colonial logics we've struggled with so far. What happens when you enfranchise not-properly humans into your citizenry, those who by their heredity are supposed to have no capacity to reason? Does democracy get destroyed? That is the founding question of the subfield of political behavior.

–3–
Political Behavior

What makes people vote the way that they do? What makes a person a conservative, liberal, or a leftist? Can people change their voting behavior or ideological tendencies? If so, how, and why? Political scientists address these questions by exploring a stunning range of stimuli that might affect behavior. For instance, perhaps you are more to the "right" in your adult life if you were taught the "authoritarian" values of obedience and respect in your childhood. Perhaps, even, some of the genes that you inherited from your parents might dispose you more toward different ideologies.

The subfield of political behavior seeks to uncover how the citizen engages with the democratic process and the degree to which its political system is responsive to that engagement. In this respect, the subfield betrays an underlying ethical commitment to democracy: a study of political behavior might help ensure that democracy works as it ideally should. The ideal, here, assumes that competent citizens are rational individuals who can make choices that best suit their interests and who receive sufficient information that enables them to do so.

But few scholars have believed that the ideal condition obtains. In fact, ever since the late nineteenth century a palpable fear has existed that not all citizens might meet the ideal of "normal" behavior. Instead, many scholars have argued that political behavior might be driven by emotions and by group interests, especially when it comes to ethnic, religious, and racially defined groups. Henceforth, much work in the subfield has searched for causes or modifiers of behavior which lie in the psychological, environmental, and even genetic realms.

"Heredity" refers to the passing on of traits from one generation to the next. This chapter shows how a logic of race heredity is foundational to the subfield of political behavior. In a historical context defined by both expanding empire and industrial urbanization, the late nineteenth-century UK and USA experienced increased internal and external movement and mixing of peoples. In response, the science of race heredity attributed the inheritance of degenerative abnormal behaviors to some races and the inheritance of "normal" political behavior to the white Anglo-Saxon race. The study of political behavior sought to mitigate the disorderly effects on the demos caused by population moving and the mixing of heredities. Arguably, this concern is still with us today.

In the first part of this chapter, I will introduce the science of race heredity within a context defined both by expansions in Britain's imperium (the areas under imperial domination) and urban industrialization in its heartland. I will then reconceptualize the beginnings of the subfield of political behavior by paying special attention to Walter Bagehot, editor-in-chief of the famous magazine the *Economist*. It is often forgotten that Bagehot was one of the first writers to apply race heredity to an explanation of political behavior via an analysis of Britain's "unwritten" constitution – that is the set of conventional norms, practices, and institutions that underpinned political administration. In his analysis, Bagehot distinguished the genius of the Anglo-Saxon race in its ability to pursue an orderly democracy. This ability, though, required guarding against the degeneration of the race.

In the next part I will turn to the late nineteenth-century US context, defined, similarly, by imperial expansion, increased immigration, and industrial urbanization. Here I will examine how the British science of race heredity was mobilized to address concerns for national unity and the preservation of Anglo-Saxon heritage. I will reconceptualize the academic and political career of President Woodrow Wilson as part of this mobilization, specifically his attempt to apply Bagehot's analysis of political behavior to the US congressional system. I will then explore the American psychologist John Watson's critique of eugenics. His "behaviorist" approach claimed that any individual could learn new behavior through environmental changes. However, I will show that Watson re-coded inherited genetics as inherited "cultural" characteristics. Therefore, both Wilson and Watson explained political behavior through the logic of race heredity – a racialized distinction between competent and incompetent citizens, normal and abnormal behavior.

After bringing the study of political behavior in US political science up to date, I will turn to Frantz Fanon. A citizen of France, hailing from the Caribbean island of Martinique, Fanon is famous for his support of Algerian independence from France, and for his blisteringly anti-colonial book, *The Wretched of the Earth*. In actual fact, Fanon trained as a clinical psychiatrist and most of his written work was in this profession. I will show how his clinical practice provides an anti-colonial reimagining of political behavior. Instead of accepting a racialized distinction between normal/abnormal behavior and competent/incompetent citizens, Fanon sought to repair the egos and psyches of those who had been made abnormal and categorized as incompetent by the structures of colonial rule.

The Science of Race Heredity

Overseas English imperialism began in the mid sixteenth century with the setting up of plantations in Ireland. By the mid nineteenth century, a new issue started to capture Britain's imperial imagination. White emigrants now populated a series of settler colonies from Canada to New Zealand, living far from "home," but not too far from indigenous peoples. Were these emigrants still of the same home stock?

This question of inheritance was increasingly directed to the population of Britain itself after Ireland joined a United Kingdom in 1801. In the 1840s, Ireland suffered a devastating famine that led to an increased rate of emigration into Britain's growing industrial towns. But were the Irish – those old colonial subjects – even white?

Given all this geographical expansion and demographic "contamination," some scholars began to look more closely at the nature of British heredity, of what it was comprised, and how it might be preserved. In 1849, John Mitchell Kemble, a historian of early medieval England and Teutonic languages, used the race science of physiognomy (the study of facial features and expressions) to assert that an Anglo-Saxon "type" could be observed in distinction to a Celtic type (Irish, Scottish) and other populations living in Britain's imperium – the areas under imperial domination (Young 2008).

The mixing of racial types was accompanied by another fear: the degeneration of the Anglo-Saxon race due to industrial urbanization. Back in 1798, Reverend Thomas Malthus had written an incredibly influential *Essay on the Principle of Population*. Therein, Malthus (1798, 48) argued pessimistically that population increased faster than food supplies, and that this demographic fact inevitably pitted "tribe" against "tribe" in a "struggle for existence."

Malthus wrote in the context of a predominantly rural and agricultural society. But by the mid nineteenth century, the struggle that Malthus portended seemed to be occurring far more viciously in industrial towns. For many observers at the time, migration from the countryside into these towns was changing the very composition of the Anglo-Saxon race. Philanthropists claimed that as rural artisans faced the squalor and poverty of urban life their moral and intellectual capacities began to degenerate. It was not at all uncommon to associate urbanization with racial degeneration. For instance, William Booth (1890, 11–12, 16), founder of the Salvation Army, worried that in the urban slums a "darkest England" existed just as did a "darkest Africa."

In these ways, race heredity emerged in the 1850s as a

key issue for the politics of empire. Commentators regularly opined that the Anglo-Saxon inheritance (whatever that might be) was being threatened by its mixing with other races as well as by the degeneration of its own "stock." This was the context in which a set of English authors published work that radically altered academic and political debates about the nature of humanity.

After returning from his global voyages in 1836, Darwin happened to read Malthus's essay on population. This intellectual encounter led him to develop a theory of "natural selection," which he published in 1859 as *On the Origin of Species by Means of Natural Selection, or the Preservation of Favoured Races in the Struggle for Life*. By this theory, Darwin sought to explain the diversity of species in terms of Malthus's "struggle for existence." Those "individuals" who inherited traits better suited to their environment would survive and reproduce whereas those who did not have such traits would cease to reproduce.

You'll have heard of Darwin. But you might not be aware of the fact that *Origin* had very little to say about the human species itself. Indeed, *Origin* did nothing to address one of the most discussed elements of human heredity in the eighteenth and nineteenth centuries – the formation and transmission of "habit" (Camic 1986). In the eighteenth century, the debate on what made people commit to particular routines of action was largely a moralistic one. But by Darwin's time, the inheritance and transmission of habit was being examined quite differently in terms of the interaction of behavior, biology, and environment.

On this topic, the French naturalist Jean-Baptiste Lamarck was far more influential than Darwin. In a book entitled *Philosophie Zoologique* (1809), Lamarck put forward his theory of "the inheritance of acquired characteristics," which was comprised of two biological claims. Firstly, the use of an organ leads to its development and strengthening, and the disuse of an organ leads to its deterioration and weakening. Secondly, individuals transmit to their progeny the results of this use or disuse.

Above all, Lamarck's theory of inheritance offered a

possibility that was absent in Darwin's mindless struggle for survival: the human might distinguish itself from other species by the use and enlargement, over time, of its brain – the organ of reason. Those who made this argument hoped that habit might turn over generations into innate instinct, upon which even more complex habits could then be developed over generations, in turn becoming new instinct, and so on and so forth. Unlike other species, human evolution demonstrated a growing intellectual capacity to control the environment.

Perhaps the most influential scholar to develop an evolutionary framework through which to understand humanity itself was Herbert Spencer. A biologist and philosopher, Spencer acknowledged that Malthus's theory of a "struggle for existence" could not explain how Europeans, at least, had evolved so quickly in the development of tools, thereby enabling mastery of their natural and social environment. To address this puzzle, Spencer turned to Lamarck's theory of the inheritance of acquired characteristics. Spencer proposed that nature – at least when it came to humans – had an inbuilt progressive tendency to build more and more complex instincts and habits, thereby enhancing and expanding the nervous system over generations.

In his 1852 essay, *A Theory of Population*, Spencer argued that increased intelligence tended to produce a complex social division of labor. Within this division, some people could specialize in perfecting moral and technical systems of self-regulation and self-control. These systems would, eventually, liberate humanity from its prior limitations, thereby refuting Malthus's pessimistic outlook. Spencer believed his own historical era to be at this tipping point.

Francis Galton, the coiner of the term "eugenics," also started questioning the implications of Darwin's theory of "natural selection" for the human species (see Kevles 1985). Success in the "struggle for existence" was proven, Galton proposed, by an organism's ability to produce offspring in abundance. But that was the problem. In British society at the time, those with the largest families were increasingly the poorer urban classes, who reproduced on the presumption that some of their children would die prematurely. Given this demographic tendency, Galton wondered whether the natural evolutionary future of humanity was degenerative. Might not the rich decrease (with their wealth, good habits, and health) and the poor increase (with their poverty, ignorance, and disease)?

After reading Darwin's *Origin*, Galton decided that it could be possible to undertake "artificial" selection by encouraging the breeding of those people considered genetically superior while dissuading the genetically inferior from reproducing. He labelled this science after the Greek "eu" (good) "genēs" (born) – good breeding. Galton first presented eugenics in an 1865 essay on *Hereditary Talent and Character*. There, he argued that the mental competencies of individuals were inherited from their parents. General ability, he claimed, was not an outcome of social circumstance (e.g. growing up in poverty) or of environment broadly conceived, but of heredity – who your parents were.

That sounds a lot like Spencer, right? But unlike Spencer, Galton suggested that habits were for the most part socially learned rather than inherited. This small difference in opinion led to a big difference in prescription. While Spencer trusted the natural evolutionary process, Galton did not. In order to ensure that civilization would not be sacrificed by the natural propensity of poor and genetically inferior people to reproduce, Galton advocated for the intentional promotion and demotion of various blood lines.

All these responses ultimately led Darwin to acknowledge that his thesis of natural selection did not work for humanity the way it did for other species. Human evolution was a special case. Tellingly, by the time he wrote his *Descent of Man* in 1871, Darwin had shifted his criteria for species "fitness" (a term he took from Spencer) from fecundity to intelligence (see Claeys 2000).

For all thinkers, though, the specificity of the human condition required an engagement with differences within the species laid out along the lines of race. In the *Descent of Man*, Darwin (1871, 1: 239, 162) admitted that phenotypical differences between "races of man" – for example, skin color – were unimportant *except* for "intellectual and moral or social faculties." Moreover, welfare provisions for the poor in civilized societies might lead to the "degeneration of a domestic race." Meanwhile, Spencer (1852, 498–500) argued that an increase in the nervous center had led the crania of Englishmen to be larger than those of Africans, Malays, and (aboriginal) Australians. The "survival of the fittest" for Spencer, was a group, not individual, struggle comprised of "families and races." Finally, Galton (1865, 320) believed he could adduce inherited character from facial features that also marked "different races of men," for example, Mongolians, Jews, negroes, gypsies, and American Indians.

We've covered a lot of ground quickly. So, here's the key point that underlies all the detail. While Darwin, Spencer, and Galton differed on the mechanisms and consequences of inheritance and evolution, all of them eventually asserted that mental fitness differed between human groups. What's more, all of them proposed that the human struggle envisioned by Malthus took place between races.

The science of heredity was avowedly a race science. In some ways, Kant's anthropology of race pre-empted the new science. Empire and colonial rule were fundamentally implicated in the race logics of this science via concerns for the integrity of the Anglo-Saxon race as it emigrated to the four corners of the earth and as urbanization in the imperial center mixed populations within a dysgenic industrial landscape. Thus, the science of race heredity grew in order to address the particular challenges accompanying Britain's empire and industrial predominance. In this context, as in the US context to which we'll turn presently, the colonial logic underpinning the study of political behavior was expressed as a logic of race heredity.

The direct translation of the science of race heredity into the study of politics was first accomplished by Walter Bagehot, an influential commentator and editor-in-chief of the *Economist*. (The magazine still has a current affairs column named after him.) Between 1865 and 1867, Bagehot published *The English Constitution* in serial form. In these years, parliamentary reform led to the enfranchisement of the skilled working class – those who now increasingly appeared in towns and cities. Accompanying reform was a concern among many of the political elite that even the "upper layer" of the working class lacked the intellect and temperament to take part in politics without creating havoc and disorder. Bagehot's serialized publication was central to this debate.

Bagehot divided the unwritten "constitution" into two parts. On one side, the parliamentary House of Lords and the monarchy comprised the "dignified" aspect of politics. For Bagehot, the value of this dignity lay in its "theatrical" element. Upper-class pomp and pageantry inspired deference in the lower-class masses. Pomp and pageantry also diverted their attention from the "efficient" sites wherein legislative decisions and executive actions actually occurred – the House of Commons and the executive cabal known as the Cabinet.

Bagehot was principally concerned with the impact of a greater inclusion of the masses into the "efficient" aspect of government. He worried, for instance, that the Reform Act (1867) would cheapen the "dignified" aspect of politics, make its theatre irrelevant, and consequently weaken the deference of the masses. However, in the second edition of *The English Constitution*, written just after the passing of the Reform Act, Bagehot (1873b, 2: 3–5) struck a much more positive tone. British politics, he decided, had already been experiencing a slow inter-generational change. In making this judgment, Bagehot drew upon Spencer's evolutionary theory. And we can see this influence clearly in another book that Bagehot began to serialize in the same year as the Reform Act.

Physics and Politics examined political behavior by direct reference to race heredity. Evolution, Bagehot claimed, had created different brain capacities among the races, which enabled and outlawed different political behaviors. In the case of the "modern savage," the mind was "tattooed over with monstrous images." Base instincts congealed in their brain's crevices such that modern savages lived a life "twisted into a thousand curious habits; his reason ... darkened by a thousand strange prejudices; his feelings ... frightened by a thousand cruel superstitions" (Bagehot 1873a, 120). (Yes, the editor-in-chief of the *Economist* really did believe this.) However, the body of the "accomplished" white man could be distinguished by the inheritance of an increasingly refined "nervous organization" that supplanted instinct with reason. In contrast to the modern savage, the brain of the European man had been smoothed over many generations by the habitual exercise of reason.

Bagehot believed this particular evolution of reason to be a moral feat. Human instincts, Bagehot admitted, were originally shared across all races. Yet the formation of cultured habits required an original and unique "action of the will," which put into effect a slow "hereditary drill" that allowed reason to conquer instinct. Whites alone had demonstrated the original will power that evolved the human mind. Other races, Bagehot asserted, possessed no "inherited creed" by virtue of which an orderly society could congeal. Moreover, the lack of will power and reason in non-white races could not be ameliorated by a program of cultural assimilation. "Imitation," Bagehot (1873a, 107) opined, "would no more make a negro out of a Brahmin, or a red-man out of an Englishman, than washing would change the spots of a leopard or the colour of an Ethiopian." Consequently, even the social mixing of races was immoral.

Bagehot developed this evolutionary theory to explain the emergence and longevity of parliament. Remember Lamarck's theory that inheritance was predicated upon the inter-generational use or non-use of an organ. Recall also how Spencer directed this theory toward the evolution of human reason. Well, in Bagehot's opinion, the "efficient" part of parliament exercised the Anglo-Saxon race's collective organ of intelligence due to the fact that so many of the political issues entertained by the House of Commons and Cabinet were matters of abstract principle. At the same time, the "dignified" element of government remediated the harmful instincts that still lurked in the lesser pedigree of the race – the lower classes. The theatrics of pomp and pageantry could transform these disorderly irrationalities into orderly deference to the upper classes. By these means, civilizational advance could proceed in an orderly fashion – and that was the unique nature of Anglo-Saxon democracy.

Let's summarize Bagehot's theory of political behavior.

Firstly, his moral opprobrium over the mixing of different races reflected wider fears regarding Anglo-Saxon purity. Secondly, his distinction between the "dignified" and the "efficient" elements of government addressed worries over the degeneration of the Anglo-Saxon "stock" brought about by industrial urbanization. In both these ways, Bagehot deployed the race logic of heredity science to make sense of political behavior and to identify ways in which the enlargement of democracy did not diminish the genius of the race.

Eugenics and Behaviorism in the United States

Similar concerns about race inter-mixture and degeneration also abounded in late nineteenth-century US society. Just like Britain, the US faced a set of transformative challenges both domestically and internationally. Domestically, the 14th amendment to the Constitution in 1868 finally codified peoples as a permanent part of the citizenry, even though "Jim Crow" discriminatory laws flourished at the local and state levels of government. The Dawes Act of 1887 marked the high point of appropriation of native American land through the reservation system. Throughout the same time period, industrialization caused significant internal migrations to the large urban conurbations of the north.

Internationally, European immigration to the US shifted away from Anglo-Saxons toward more southern and eastern Europeans, bringing populations considered by many to be inferior in terms of their religious denominations, social habits, skills, and values. This Atlantic movement was matched, in the popular imaginary, with migration across the Mexican border by peoples who were said to bring with them radical ideas of labor organizing. Both immigrations intersected with internal migrations in ways that seemed to make urban areas hotbeds of disorder. At the same time, the US empire expanded further beyond the continent as the Spanish–American war in 1898 delivered new colonial possessions – lands and peoples – in the Philippines, Guam, and Puerto Rico, with Hawai'i annexed in the same year. All in all, then, as the US expanded its imperium, the population incorporated within its borders seemed to be more and more fractured along racial lines, and more at risk of social and physical degeneration, especially in the growing urban areas. Given all this fracturing and degenerating, could one continue to believe in the hundred-year-old conceit of the Declaration of Independence that a "social contract" between fictitious equals held the polity together (Heinze 2003)?

In this context, the British science of race heredity helped many academics and politicians explain and prescribe remedies to the problem of national unity. And perhaps the most influential movement to adopt this race science was progressivism (Leonard 2017).

Progressivists worried that a proliferation of isolated immigrant groups would be fertile grounds for a "spoils system" through which immoral politicians could carve out fiefdoms and corrupt public office. This system, progressivists claimed, would only intensify the increase in private interests that already accompanied industrial urbanization. For these reasons, progressivists feared that external mixing and internal degeneracy threatened the delicate colonial experiment of transplanting Anglo-Saxon democracy across the Atlantic. The solution, they argued, was to find ways to unify the polity by uplifting the masses into a homogenized middle class. Toward this aim, many progressivists advocated eugenics.

When the American Political Science Association (APSA) was formed in 1903, its founders were mostly progressivists (see Blatt 2018). Many prominent members sought to evaluate the determinants of political behavior across a racially fractured polity. Their aim was to develop policies that might help to sculpt such behavior into a shape commensurate with Anglo-Saxon democracy.

But we're getting ahead of ourselves. Because, before 1903, political science was conventionally associated with the study of history. And it is here that the British science of race heredity was first picked up by the American intelligentsia. To tell this story I need to take you to the early days of my own institution, Johns Hopkins University.

The founding purpose of Hopkins, opened in Baltimore in 1876, was to provide a graduate education to a public-spirited middle class intent on social, economic, and political reform. The opening address of the university signaled this project, provided, as it was, by "Darwin's bulldog" T. H. Huxley, who was known for his vociferous promotion of evolution. In this spirit of reform, Hopkins was the first university in the US to provide its own doctoral degree, although its first president, Daniel Gilman, began this independence from Europe by transplanting German academic practices as well as German-trained American faculty into Baltimore.

One such academic was Herbert Baxter Adams, hired as a fellow in history. Recall the English historian John Kemble, who I mentioned above. Adams was inspired by Kemble's "Teutonism," which tracked Anglo-Saxon culture back to the self-governing villages of ancient Germany. Adams (1882) extended Kemble's mythic history forward so as to claim that the source of American democracy lay in the Anglo-Saxon settlers who, having crossed the Atlantic, set up the same kind of communities in New England.

In fine, Adams considered democracy to be a racial inheritance. As head of the Hopkins department of History and Political Science, Adams saw his task not only as promoting the study of local histories, but as using these studies to train a new school of administrators and public officials. He hoped that these officials might transfer the ethos of Anglo-Saxon-influenced local government into the halls of national government.

Enter Woodrow Wilson. You'll have come across Wilson, perhaps, as an exemplary "liberal internationalist" – the great promoter of a lasting peace at the end of World War I, and a co-progenitor of the League of Nations, the institution that was supposed to guarantee the global peace. But you might not know that prior to this Wilson had made a name for himself in political science as a scholar who advanced the study of public administration (see Blatt 2018, chapter 2).

Wilson arrived at Hopkins in 1883 as a graduate student. Like Adams, and the progressivist movement, Wilson worried that the nation was degenerating and that its salvation lay not in the social contract but in the integrity of inherited affiliations. The US division of powers, argued Wilson, exacerbated the externally and internally induced fractures evident in the American polity. The many committees that featured in the congressional system, in Wilson's view, encouraged sectarian differences that were already degenerating the body politic.

In pursuing his critique of the American congressional system, Wilson took inspiration from Bagehot's *English Constitution*. Specifically, Wilson presented the parliamentary model, with its more efficient concentration of executive and legislative power, as better suited to the forging of a strong unified nation. Also evident in Wilson's thought was the influence of Bagehot's *Physics and Politics*.

Like Adams, Wilson believed that American democracy could be understood as a "truly organic growth," originating in Teutonic forests, and carried across the seas by Anglo-Saxon settlers to take root in the villages of New England. Agreeing with Bagehot, and sharing his concern for orderly change, Wilson proposed that the genius of the Anglo-Saxon race – even when transplanted to a new continent – was its ability to balance both vigor and rationality, so as to induce an evolutionary development of political behavior. The "effective" and "dignified" elements of government allowed rational deliberation and rash instincts to be balanced so as to produce an "animated moderation."

Writing in the *Political Science Quarterly*, a journal run by John Burgess (another Teutonist), Wilson directed his Bagehot-inspired thesis explicitly toward fears of racial mixing. Unlike the Anglo-Saxon race, the bulk of mankind, asserted Wilson, was "rigidly unphilosophical." Echoing Bagehot's concerns over working-class enfranchisement, Wilson sounded the alarm that "nowadays the bulk of mankind votes." As if that was not enough, these masses were no longer only Anglo-Saxons, but also "Irishmen," "negroes," and others. To govern effectively in this context required the ability to "influence minds cast in every mould of race, minds inheriting every bias of environment" (Wilson 1887, 209).

Wilson thus conceived of the challenge of public administration through a logic of race heredity that required the evolved Anglo-Saxon mind to be preserved amid the contamination of the public sphere by degenerate racial inheritances. In place of the British parliament, Wilson ultimately presented the presidency as the force that would bind a fractured nation together and make sure that Congress remained honest. To be such a force, Wilson envisaged the president as the chief educator of public opinion.

Members of the Rastafari movement call politics "politricks." As Wilson moved from education into politics he began to temper his rhetoric, presenting the same logics of race heredity but now in the language of civics. This led to Wilson's political career being associated by many with a liberal disposition that in fact masked his ongoing commitment to preserving Anglo-Saxon heredity at the heart of government.

Take, for instance, Wilson's relationship with African Americans. Actually, Wilson had always been suspicious of the emancipation won from America's Civil War. "It was a menace to society itself," he argued, "that the negroes should all of a sudden be set free and left without tutelage or restraint" (Ambrosius 2007, 690). Just like Bagehot, Wilson was deeply distrustful of the ability of the "negro" mind to exercise rationality.

As president of Princeton University, Wilson encouraged the de facto barring of African American applicants to the student body, arguing that a "negro" presence would be out of keeping with "the whole temper and tradition of the place" (O'Reilly 1997, 117). When Wilson became President of the United States, he imported the segregation policy of his Princeton days into his White House administration. Wilson surreptitiously undertook a "plan of concentration," which made sure that black and white workers would not "mix" in any one bureau of the administration (Ambrosius 2007, 699).

As President in the White House, Wilson channeled progressivist concerns over race mixing into immigration policy. "We cannot," he claimed in the language of Bagehot's evolutionary theory, "make a homogenous population out of people who do not blend with the Caucasian race" (Vought 1994, 29). Wilson was kinder to the putatively white (but not Anglo-Saxon) populations from southern and eastern Europe, yet still suspicious of those whose political allegiances suggested a hyphenated identity – e.g. Italian-Americans.

Remember that in this era the fear of race degeneration spoke to both immigration and industrial urbanization – an outward-facing fear of race mixing, and an inward-facing concern for the growing power of degenerative masses. Tellingly, when it came to the naturalization of European immigrants, Wilson was keen to remove them from cities and relocate them to small and rural communities. He trusted that the Anglo-Saxon inheritance in those communities remained in a purer form than would be found in industrialized cities. Away from dysgenic conurbations, Wilson hoped that new immigrants could avail themselves of the Anglo-Saxon inheritance and learn political behaviors appropriate to their new status as Americans.

Wilson's image of the presidency as an impartial paternal figure rising above sectarian interests to effect social change was congruent to the progressivist ideology that he aligned himself with. So too was his belief that at least some of humanity had malleable heritage and that their behavior could be shaped by their environment. Wilson thereby mobilized the race logics of hereditary science to set up an abiding distinction between competent and incompetent citizens, and normal and abnormal behavior.

But if Wilson was not a card-carrying eugenicist, progressivists by and large were, and they reserved the right to use eugenics to redress the degeneration of the Anglo-Saxon race when necessary. I imagine that this might surprise you. We often imagine eugenics to be a project only supported by Nazis, not pursued in so-called "progressive" politics. But eugenics, after Galton, was widely promoted as a capstone science of humanity. Plenty of governments outside of Germany developed eugenicist programs.

The first eugenicist-inspired sterilization law in the US was passed by Indiana in 1907. Four years later, biologist Charles Davenport founded the Eugenics Record Office in Cold Spring Harbor, New York. Producing data that suggested certain races and ethnicities were of "low intelligence" and prone to "feeble-mindedness," eugenicists such as Davenport became extremely influential in politics. In 1924, Congress passed a blatantly racist immigration act that even Wilson partly balked at.

I've focused on eugenicists because their prevalence in politics at this moment in time leads us to an engagement with the social scientific method that is actually named after the study of behavior. In part, "behaviorism" rose to prominence in the early twentieth century as a challenge to eugenics. To tell this part of the story we once more need to return to Hopkins, but this time to John Broadus Watson who in 1908 was made chair of the psychology department.

Watson was initially a student of animal behavior but he increasingly sought to apply his findings to human behavior. Watson took issue with those, such as Bagehot, who imagined that the shape of the brain somehow determined intellectual faculties. He also had little time for Spencer's claims about the evolution of consciousness. Watson did embrace the progressivist ethos but refuted the science of race heredity. He argued instead that behavior was determined by a reaction to external or internal stimuli which triggered either fear, rage, or love. By focusing solely on the environment in which an organism lived, Watson believed that it was eminently possible not only to explain and predict all behavior but to control and change it.

In 1924, and in good part as a response to the eugenics-inspired immigration act of the same year, Watson released a manifesto entitled *Behaviorism*. In this landmark publication, Watson (1924, 77) dismissed the idea that "capacity, talent, temperament, mental constitution, and characteristics" were inherited, least of all through racial lineages. In doing so, he famously challenged the attribution of criminality and "feeble-mindedness" to genetic inheritance:

Give me a dozen healthy infants well formed, and my own specified world to bring them up in and I will guarantee to take any one at random and train him to become any type of specialist I might select regardless of his talents, penchants, tendencies, abilities, vocations, and race of his ancestors. (Watson 1924, 82)

Watson therefore refuted eugenics by proposing that anyone, regardless of heritage, was entirely capable of developing behavioral patterns that were in keeping with "the mandates of society" and supportive of democratic politics. He advocated for artificial selection, if you like, but strictly of the environmental rather than genetic kind.

Let's pause for a minute. Because I want to point out something about the meaning of science when applied to the human world. For Watson, the *means* of behaviorist inquiry were certainly "scientific," that is, value neutral: laboratory experiments on animal and human subjects could document, evaluate, and replicate the varied responses to stimuli. Yet when it came to humans, the *ends* of such inquiry were clearly normative, that is, value laden. Watson (1924, 284) believed that behaviorism could lay "a foundation for saner living," as a "science that prepares men and women for understanding the first principles of their own behavior," leading them to "rearrange their own lives," and "prepare themselves to bring up their own children in a healthy way."

At regular points in this book we'll revisit the value-laden underbelly of science. But for now, I want you to consider that Watson's science had conservative aims. For him, existing social conventions formed the baseline of behavioral normality. And while Watson (1924, 144) accepted that baselines changed over time, he believed that behaviorism would help to guide changes so that they did not eventuate in "too rapid lessening of control." In other words, Watson shared with Bagehot and Wilson a concern that responsible elites should not lose control of the levers of societal changes lest they were to open the floodgates of mass disorder.

Principal among the challenges to convention that concerned Watson were the status of women and the weakening of marriage and church ties. As an aside, it's ironic that Watson became personally unstuck when he tested the speed of social change. In 1920 he was fired from Hopkins due to his lack of contriteness when it was discovered that he had been having an affair with Rosalie Rayner, one of his graduate students at the time.

Anyway, there's no doubt that despite being conservative, Watson's behaviorism re-affirmed the universalism of the human condition in stark contrast to the science of heredity, which depicted evolution as the struggle between races for survival. Despite all this, though, I want to argue that Watson's social conservatism also betrayed a similar logic to the science of heredity, namely, that races developed qualitatively differently.

In the last chapter I noted that the term "phenotype" refers to the presentation of observable characteristics. I added that, scientifically speaking, such characteristics can include behaviors as well as looks, and that the two have more often than not been conceptually entangled. Just think about Kant's claim that you are stupid because you are black. To put it bluntly: just because you talk about culture doesn't mean that you're not still evaluating humans through race logic.

Case in point, Watson. Like so many "non-racist" scholars of the twentieth century, Watson took the supposedly biological characteristics associated with race and re-presented them as cultural behaviors. He implicitly ranked these cultural attributes in a hierarchy of values. At the top were cultures that valued rationality, because only through a rational, scientific approach could you change behaviors and save democracy. That's why Watson proposed that less culturally developed humans – for instance "Australian tribes" – demonstrated less complex stimuli-responses than the "educated European" (Watson 1913).

Watson believed that different "cultural" capacities for behavioral response were especially problematic when it came to childhood development. He was particularly concerned that irrational habits learned in one's early years could seriously diminish the ability to react rationally to stimuli in adult life. Watson's prime example of malformed childhood development focused on the putative fact that African Americans, unlike whites, held onto a belief in myth and the supernatural. "Colored nurses down South," Watson (1924, 3) proposed, "have gained control over the young white children by telling them that there is someone ready to grab them in the dark." Such irrationalities formed behavioral habits that the adult was burdened with in his public and professional life.

In fine, Watson's attempt to moderate political behavior also had racial determinates – albeit cultural not genetic. Even as he sought to refute the science of race heredity, Watson used its logic to set up another kind of cultural-instead-of-biological racialized distinction between competent and incompetent citizens, and normal and abnormal behavior.

In the introduction to this chapter I described political behavior as a study of the way in which competent citizens react to and take part in the political process. We've just tracked how the study of political behavior emerged as part of a concern for domestic and international migration, its degenerate effect on the competent (Anglo-Saxon) citizen, and the corresponding disorder and abnormal behavior it might infect the democratic process with. In all this, a eugenic response vied with a behavioral response. The two academic positions were opposed, no doubt. But both depicted the competent/incompetent citizen through a set of racial inheritances that set normal or abnormal behavior, whether culturally or genetically.

Shortly, I'm going to show you how Frantz Fanon radically challenges the distinction between competent and incompetent citizens through his anti-colonial psychiatric practice. Before that, it might be instructive to follow the routes through which behavioral and biological approaches to behavior find their way into our present-day study of political science and how the logics of race heredity have and have not changed.

Charles Merriam, who in 1900 became the first member of the political science faculty at Chicago University, was a progressivist, a mild proponent of the eugenics movement, and also a subscriber to behaviorism. In his eyes, all these approaches spoke of a "practical" rather than theoretical approach to the study of political behavior. The practical – or "scientific" – approach came to define the "Chicago School" of political science that he founded.

But what was the nature of the political problems that Merriam hoped "scientific knowledge," as he put it, could solve? In an address to the American Political Science Association (APSA) in 1925, Merriam (1926, 8) spoke of the need to engage "basic problems" such as crime, alcoholism, "the vexed question of human migration [and] the relations of the negro." He also proposed that APSA deliberate on how "modern scientific doctrines regarding heredity and eugenics [might have a] bearing upon the foundations of our political and economic order" (see also Hanchard 2018).

In particular moments of history, time seems to speed up: profound challenges and transformations happen one after the other. Take the end of World War II. The Shoah (Jewish holocaust) displaced – and in some instances delegitimized – the notion that political behavior could or should be engineered in any way. However, this delegitimization did not last long. Just a few years after the end of the war, a Cold War started between capitalist and communist powers. In this new context, a "science of behavior" seemed to better convey a commitment to making democracy work. The label "social science" sounded, well, socialist and dangerously totalitarian (Gunnell 2013). It's difficult to imagine the incredible sensitivity that accompanied these labels at the time. But a political campaign called "McCarthyism" sought to expose anyone who had any communist sympathies as "un-American" and potentially treasonous.

In the early days of the Cold War, a political scientist at Chicago University called David Easton rekindled Merriam's aspirations, absent of their eugenicist leanings and in response to the atrocities of World War II. Easton presented "behavioralism" (note the slight change in spelling) as an alternative to "political theory." In his first ever publication, Easton associated "theory" with a number of German émigré intellectuals who, in his opinion, questioned the basic premise of liberal democratic politics. While Easton found this rejection of liberal ideology extremely worrying, he admitted that a purely idealistic liberalism did not in any way accord with reality.

To resolve this conundrum Easton turned to none other than Walter Bagehot. In Easton's opinion, Bagehot had presented a "realistic" defense of liberalism. Recall that Bagehot did not believe that the masses had the same competencies to rule as elites did. Now, while not invoking Bagehot's racism, Easton (1949, 18–19, 23) nevertheless accepted that within the citizenry existed an uneven inheritance of instinct and habits. Mindful of this supposed fact, Easton hoped that the "scientific method" could be wielded to illuminate "social facts about sources of political power."

After Easton's early interventions, behavioralism in political science came to refer to an anti-ideology method of scientific inquiry – the use of statistical or experimental data to derive hypotheses on repeatable behaviors. Yet the socially conservative aims of this science of behavior, which Watson had held to in the inter-war period, arguably remained. The baseline commitment to an incremental change of democratic norms was now pursued as part of a Cold War defense against the degenerate nature of Communism. Considering the late nineteenth-century context in which a concern for political behavior grew, it's important to note that anti-communism was often joined with anti-blackness and xenophobia (Burden-Stelly 2017).

Behavioralism continued to focus on environmental factors. But what about the biological factors that were so important to eugenics? Cue Harold Laswell, who trained for his PhD with Merriam at Chicago University. As a professor at Yale University, Lasswell reintroduced the study of biology in his 1956 presidential address to APSA. Eugenics was, at this moment in time, still a discredited pursuit. So Lasswell carefully urged for more training of political scientists in the growing field of genetics, which had recently regained some credibility by producing the first model of DNA.

By the late 1960s, the study of "biopolitics" had become a regular feature of political science. Albert Somit, another

Chicago graduate, embraced work in neurobiology, physiology and psychopharmacology as proof that it was possible to directly influence and control human behavior. Somit (1972) identified the source of this behavioral control in genetically transmitted patterns of response that had developed over millennia – such as fight, flight, territoriality, male bonding, and so on.

Wait. That's not a million miles always from nineteenth-century race science, right? Well, whether that's a fair observation or not, what is undisputable is that this era saw the return of eugenics in American intellectual life. Much of this resurgence was to do with the fact that, in response to the black-led freedom movement, President Lyndon Johnson pushed through not only the Civil Rights Act but also a set of public measures designed to tackle some of the structural causes of poverty and inequality. These measures, associated with a "war on poverty," had to necessarily target racial disparities (see Raz 2013).

In response, the educational psychologist and eugenicist Arthur Jensen argued that 80 percent of intelligence was genetically inherited and that programs such as Johnson's, which assumed along behavioral lines that environmental influences might redress racial inequalities, were wasting taxpayer dollars. By the 1970s, eugenicists were sounding the alarm that all the degenerative influences that their early twentieth-century counterparts claimed made democracy unworkable had returned: poverty, crime, alcoholism, and mental illness.

Since the 1970s, more and more political scientists have proposed that an evolutionary struggle between different groups plays out in the public sphere. Worryingly, despite the human genome map conclusively demonstrating that, at the level of DNA, race does not exist, race still continues to be smuggled into such evolutionary analysis (Duster 1990). Phenotypically presented behaviors clearly underpin much public and political rhetoric of contemporary populism, and can range from the avowedly racist to the culturally descriptive. You'll no doubt be familiar with these kinds of propositions. Here are some examples that, while fabricated, are quite resonant with contemporary headlines: "Muslims can't detach religion from science"; "Chinese parents keep their kids under strict control"; "Blacks suffer from a welfare syndrome"; "Mexicans are drug dealers."

Meanwhile, much academic and popular attention continues to be attracted to the identification of particular genes that govern political attitudes and behavior. "Genopolitics" has provocatively argued that even ideology has a strong basis in genetic inheritance (for example, Fowler and Dawes 2013). These arguments have gained perhaps the most media attention in our partisan era, garnering headlines in the popular press such as "our politics is in our DNA" (Junger 2019), or "can your genes predict whether you'll be a conservative or liberal" (Tuschman 2013)?

To my mind, the most worrying element of such work is the way in which, despite incredible progress in gene science, many scholars in political science tend to reproduce the logics of early twentieth-century debates. Let me now recap the journey we've taken so far, so you can get a sense of my concern.

The study of political behavior was an outgrowth of the science of race heredity – as exemplified by Bagehot and Wilson – as well as a critical response to those sciences – as exemplified by Watson. This debate revolved around two shared assumptions. Firstly, all participants explored the inheritance or modification of behavior along hierarchical lines of race, whether that line be drawn biologically – in the case of eugenics – or culturally – in the case of behaviorism. Secondly, all participants conscripted the scientific method to help paternally engineer changes in the citizenry deemed inevitable and necessary for the preservation of democracy.

Bagehot, Wilson, and Watson presumed that the white/ Anglo-Saxon man exhibited behaviour "normal" for a civilized democracy. The question, then, is whether it's possible to hold an ethical commitment to democratic change that is not dependent upon attributing differences in behavioral competency to racialized groups – the competent citizen with normal behavior versus the incompetent citizen with abnormal behavior. Can we imagine a way to promote the values of democracy – equality, freedom, accountability – without that race logic? Fanon answers, avowedly, yes.

Fanon's anti-colonial psychiatry

Ego is a term that pertains to the sense you have of yourself as a consciously thinking individual. Ego is a very important part of the psyche. Psyche is a term that pertains to the holistic formation of the self – mind, body, and spirit. Fanon argues that colonial legacies remain crucial to the psyches of French citizens – black and white. He claims that the white citizen must see her/himself as the "normal" ego in distinction to the black citizen. Alternatively, the black citizen must believe that her/his own ego is dependent upon the recognition of the white citizen. To become normal, that is, to feel oneself to be a whole person and thus a French citizen, the black person must try to become white. In short, blackness is the phenotype of an incompetent citizen – one who cannot act as an independent and responsible individual.

In the last chapter we touched upon Fanon's first major work, *Black Skins White Masks*. In that text, he goes into some detail describing how this racialization of normal behavior creates disorders in the black psyche. Stories recounted to black and white children from an early age associate blackness with "tom-toms, cannibalism, intellectual deficiency, fetishism, racial defects, slave-ships, and above all else, above all, *Y a bon banania*" (Fanon 1986, 112). This last phase pertains to a popular breakfast cereal featuring a grinning Senegalese native soldier – banania man – who is at once child-like and ferocious. Fanon suggests that, for these reasons, French citizenship takes the shape of a national split personality between the holistically formed white ego and the black malformed ego.

Fanon initially situates his argument within the Martiniquan context – an island colony in the Caribbean that in 1946 becomes incorporated as a department (a local administrative unit) of France. After serving in the army during World War II, Fanon moves to France to pursue his studies and ultimately qualifies as a clinical psychiatrist. He tries to incorporate his previous philosophical speculations into a medical practice. Basically, Fanon wants to understand ego formation as a kind of "afterlife" of colonial rule, one which produces a national split personality between colonizer and colonized.

In this undertaking, Fanon argues against scholars who believe that the malformation of egos among colonial populations is somehow a natural inheritance rather than a response to colonial rule. Addressing debates over biological inheritance versus environmental conditioning, Fanon (2018a, 520) asks whether the human brain develops as an "endogenous phenomenon" or whether it is a "social product." Fanon is inclined toward the latter position (Gibson and Beneduce 2017). And when it comes to this issue, he is especially concerned with the debates that rage over Muslim Algerians residents in France.

At this point, I need to give you a quick heads up on Algeria. France colonized the coastal areas of what is now known as Algeria in 1830 and in 1848 turned that territory into three departments of France. Although ruling over ever larger territories of Algeria, France did not grant Muslim and Jewish populations citizenship. In 1865, they were allowed to apply, yet few did as it effectively meant renouncing their right to be governed by their religious rules. In 1870, Jews – but not the Muslim majority – were automatically turned into citizens.

Given this torturous and intimate history, Muslim Algerians in France are treated with great suspicion in Fanon's time. For many white commentators, it appears as if Algerians have an irrational fear of death that paralyses them and makes them ill-fitting for French citizenship. An "Algiers School" of psychiatry calls this phenomenon the "North African syndrome." Proponents of the school determine that the Algerian displays "subcortical dominance," meaning neurological immaturity, i.e. abnormal ego development. What's more, this immaturity is ascribed to the evolutionary inheritance of the North African along the lines posed by Herbert Spencer. For instance, Fanon (2018c, 527) recounts the opinion of Professor Jean Sutter, who claims that "primitivism is not a lack of maturity, it is a social condition at the end of its evolution."

Fanon (1970, 24) counters the Algiers school. On the one hand, he argues, Algerians have been taught "in school, in the street, in the [army] barracks" that they are indeed French. On the other hand, when in mainland France, Algerians are told to "go back to their country" – which is paradoxically part of France! This cancelling of national identity on account of race is exactly what Fanon believes rules out any recognition of Algerians as fellow citizens, hence leading to the morbid fear of death – a social death.

Fanon's great annoyance arises from the fact that so-called experts attribute this pathology to a racial inheritance that they imagine to be entirely separate to the political paradox that they live in (French/not-French). Fanon (1970, 22) reports Dr. Leon Mugniery's assertion, along these lines, that:

> granting of French citizenship, conferring equality of rights, seems to have been too hasty ... rather than [based] on the fact of the social and intellectual evolution of a race having a civilization that is at times refined but still primitive in its social, family and sanitary behavior.

Doesn't this logic of race heredity remind you of Bagehot, Wilson and even Watson?

Fanon moves to Algeria in 1953 and becomes resident psychiatrist at Blida-Joinville Hospital, about 20 kilometers south west of Algiers. It will come as no surprise to you that, in his medical practice, Fanon rejects the evolutionary argument in favor of a focus on the human brain as a "social product." Normality, argues Fanon, is not an objective criterion, but one used first and foremost to underpin the colonial split of normal colonizer versus abnormal colonized.

At Blida-Joinville, Fanon urges his fellow psychiatrists to ponder the importance of social recognition in the healthy development of the psyche. If one is not considered a comparable human by other citizens, then there is no possibility of social engagement: the ego will "atrophy." Crucially, Fanon develops this therapeutic practice to account not simply for the psychological or physiological presentation of illness, but above all for the "social situation" in which it is embedded.

I mentioned above that behavioralists in the Cold War US academy appealed to science as a neutral arbiter. Fanon is by no means anti-science: after all, he is trained in the use of pharmaceutical interventions. Still, Fanon points out that when it comes to Algerians, colonialism has often used the authority of science and scientists to break communities apart. You can imagine how rational it is, in these conditions, for Muslim Algerians to identify doctors with a "monolithic block" of colonizers (Fanon 1967, 140).

Fanon is keen to redress the atrophy of the Muslim ego by bringing the social world into the hospital ward. He becomes wary of the national split personality of French citizenship that still pits colonized against colonizer. Consequently, his therapy must appeal to the cultures and faiths that are more intimate to his patients than the world of "science." "It was essential," recalls Fanon (2018b, 363), "to go from the biological level to the institutional one."

Fanon realizes that the everyday practices that will draw the ego of white female patients back into a social setting – theatre, films, music recordings, embroidery, and so on – are perceived by Muslim patients as interventions designed to break down their own community of belonging. Patients in his Muslim ward will require different "stimuli" to those in his white female ward. Fanon dares not even use interpreters in the Muslim ward: they too are perceived as agents of colonial rule. Instead, he seeks to cultivate social life by the introduction of conventional Muslim practices led by Muslims – Moorish cafés, traditional religious feasts, and professional storytellers.

The point is that Fanon does not see in the cultural practices of the "colonized" evidence of a primitive or abnormal ego that might be ill equipped with the rational behavior required for mature democratic participation. Rather, he identifies in these practices the material with which to build back in his patients a healthy psyche. In Fanon's psychiatric method, it is the very logic of inheritance that divides individuals into racialized "normal, orderly, progressive" and "abnormal, disorderly, degenerative" groups, a division which rules out the meaningful engagement of all citizens in the democratic process.

Fanon's clinical method evinces radically different assumptions to those underpinning the social sciences of Bagehot, Wilson, and Watson, all of whom variously predicated their analysis of political behavior upon the divisive logics of racial inheritance. The difference between competent citizens exhibiting normal behavior and incompetent citizens exhibiting abnormal behavior is a logic that Fanon cannot abide. In his resignation letter from Blida-Joinville Hospital, Fanon writes in protest at the increasingly violent suppression by French forces of Muslim Algerians. Addressing himself to the Resident Minister of Algeria, Fanon contrasts the democratic aspiration of anti-colonial self-determination, which his psychiatric method supports, against the un-democratic practices of colonial rule:

> The function of a social structure is to set up institutions that are traversed by a concern for humankind. A society that forces its members into desperate solutions is a non-viable society, a society that needs replacing ... No pseudo-national mystification finds grace when up against the demand to think. (Fanon 2018a, 435)

Conclusion

Race heredity, whether culturally or biologically defined, and its association with the degeneration of democracy, remains a concern in contemporary politics. True, the term Anglo-Saxon is no longer a key racial identifier, but the "English-speaking world" or "Anglosphere" (minus India) certainly is. Just think, then and now, about the disdain for Mexican migrants in the US and for eastern European migrants in Britain. Think about non-European migrants then and now, and how political discourse presents these people as degenerative of the body politics whether in terms of the oppressive religion they bring or the germs that they spread. Finally, contemplate just how persistent anti-blackness has been, whether in terms of police killings or deportations.

But, between environmental and biological heredity, I think it's fair to say that the latter has captured the current attention of political scientists far more. This raises a question: is the biological study of political behavior ever warranted? Perhaps that's the wrong question to address. As a clinician, Fanon had no fear of biology. In any case, few scholars who seriously engage with molecular biology and other such sciences nowadays pretend that genetic influences are straightforwardly determinate in the messy world of human being. For instance, John Alford, Carolyn Funk, and John Hibbing (2005) have made the case that political attitudes and behaviors are the result of both environmental and genetic factors. To put it bluntly, and, as Evan Charney and William English (2013, 12) have recently argued, when it comes to understanding complex behaviors, "genes [by themselves] are the wrong level of analysis."

Remember that Sylvia Wynter found a way to decolonize the image of the "human" with the help of biological sciences. So, rather than avoiding biology per se, I would say that we need to overturn a stubborn and long-standing logic that is so often smuggled into biological analyses of politics. I'm talking about the claim that humans are organized into races whose biological and/or cultural phenotypes demonstrate different inheritances, one of which is "normal" and the others of which are degenerately abnormal. That is Fanon's critique of psychiatry when it serves French colonialism.

In this chapter, we've recontextualized the emergence of political behavior by reference to fears of the internal and external race degeneration of the citizenry. We've reconceptualized the notion of "normal" behavior by tracking a colonial logic that inheres in the science of race heredity. We've followed that logic through the work of Bagehot, Wilson, and Watson up to contemporary genopolitics. We've reimagined political behavior by following Fanon's argument that the "norm" has only ever been promoted by attributing abnormality and degeneracy to others – both external and internal to the race/nation/citizenry. And Fanon's psychiatric practice cautions us against presuming that we can easily escape the logic of race heredity by swapping the "gene" with the "culture."

Fanon's work also forces us to consider that, when it comes to the behavior of citizens, the promotion of *the* norm has never really operated as a defense of democracy. Rather, a singular standard of normality and competency has more often than not been a profoundly undemocratic act of placing some groups over others. Putting in place, expelling, and creating second-class citizens, those who have a lesser claim on welfare, living standards and basic rights, is the outcome of such group definitions, whether intended or unintended. To safeguard democracy, or at least, the promise of individual equality and accountability, we would want to do away with the very notion of "normal" behavior, inherited or acquired.

Similar challenges have confronted political scientists, who study behavior in a scaled-up fashion, looking at the different paths of development that various states travel. The subfield of comparative politics is our next stop.

–4–

Comparative Politics

We all compare, every day. The heat, bitterness, saltiness, or sweetness of different foods; the temperament of different friends. We assess and evaluate similarities and differences in order to orient ourselves to a diverse world. Using comparisons to build knowledge of our world is at least as old as Aristotle. Comparison seems to be hardcoded into the human condition. Surely the comparative method is not an invention of European colonialism?

When it comes to political science we compare an astounding array of conditions and characteristics between different political systems. For example, comparativists explore executive, legislative, and judicial branches of multiple governments, as well as parties, and party politics, election laws, governance mechanisms, regulative bodies and norms, and territorial jurisdictions. On a broader scale, comparativists also examine the distinctions between non-democratic and democratic polities, and the varied paths of "political development" from one system to the other.

I'm going to argue that it is with regard to the idea of "development" itself that colonial logics can be identified in the comparative approach to political science. These logics have similarities to those found in the subfields of political theory and political behavior. This is especially the case regarding the racialized division of humanity into groups who are more and less competent to exercise reason for political ends. That said, the colonial logic in comparative politics has a special complexity, which I'll get to soon.

The philosophers and scholars whom we're going to examine in the first parts of this chapter accepted that human groups arranged themselves differently. They also believed that through colonization Europeans would introduce more virtuous ways of living to indigenous peoples. In this respect, they wished differences to be closed down over time, and for indigenous groups to assimilate to superior European values and practices. So, differences in political systems and cultural practices were accepted as natural to humanity only for all these systems and practices to be evaluated by reference to one universal pathway of human development. This is what I'm going to call the "colonial paradox of comparison."

A paradoxical statement or condition is one that is seemingly self-contradictory. The paradox to which I am drawing attention consists of the following: difference is accepted analytically, that is, as part of the way in which you understand human behavior; but difference is disavowed "normatively," meaning that certain values and practices are set as the norm – the standard – by which all human groups should be evaluated and prepared for assimilation. Put succinctly, the colonial paradox of comparison pertains to the seeming contradiction between (a) accepting difference as a condition of humanity but (b) disavowing certain kinds of differences as bad. This paradox is resolved with a politics of assimilation, which adjudicates who is undertaking orderly development and who is undertaking disorderly development and must be stopped.

The first part of this chapter recontextualizes the emergence of comparative analysis within the expansion of European empires and the challenges that came with maintaining them. I will begin with the conquest of the Americas and the subsequent comparisons made between the religious beliefs of indigenous peoples and Europeans. I will use this background to reconceptualize the idea of "improvement," popularized in late-eighteenth-century Scottish moral philosophy. For this purpose, I will examine the work of Adam Ferguson (1723–1816), a famous Scottish philosopher of the late eighteenth century, who argued that while all humanity "improved" their natural surroundings Europeans had found a more virtuous path that led to "commercial society" or what we nowadays call capitalism. I will then shift the colonial context of comparative analysis by following through the concern for "improvement" as it morphed into a concern for "colonial development" in the inter-war years of the twentieth century. Specifically, I will reconceptualize the idea of "development" through the work of famous anthropologist Bronislaw Malinowski (1884–1942). I will examine how he characterized the development aspirations of "native elites" as disorderly and dangerous to empire's integrity.

In the second part, I will turn to the formalization of the subfield of comparative politics at the beginning of the Cold War era. I will contextualize the work of the US-based Committee on Comparative Politics (CCP) within the struggle between the Western "free world" and the Eastern communist bloc over the fate of decolonization and the direction in which newly independent polities might develop. I mentioned above that there was a special complexity to the colonial logic utilized by comparativists. Well, the CCP utilized categories that did not directly reference colonialism but, rather, an ideal-typical snapshot of "traditional" and "modern" societies. However, I will reconceptualize this usage to demonstrate that colonial logics still paradoxically determined what counted as orderly and disorderly "modernization." I will focus on the reactivation by the committee's scholars of the old colonial fear over disorderly native elites recklessly pursuing independence.

In the third part, I will reimagine the meaning of development by moving to Tanzania. In 1967, Julius Nyerere, the leader of this newly independent state, proclaimed a development policy of self-reliance. Tanzania disputed the modernizing policies formulated and promoted by the West and in so doing attracted radical minds from across the world. I will explore the work of a group of radical scholars who taught at the Dar es Salaam University. Walter Rodney

(1942–1980), Giovani Arrighi (1937–2009), and John Saul (1938–) refused to explain developmental differences by reference to the traditional or modern characteristics of native elites. Rather, they shifted their scope of analysis to the globally unequal relations of exploitation carved out by capitalist neo-imperialism and which, they argued, delivered under-development to some and development to others.

Colonialism and the Paradox of Comparison

Let's start where Sylvia Wynter started: with the Spanish conquest of the Americas. Accompanying the first wave of Spanish settlers to Hispaniola (present day Haiti/Dominican Republic) was a man called Bartolomé de las Casas (1484–1566). After becoming a Dominican friar, Las Casas experienced a spiritual awakening and started to defend indigenous peoples from the violence meted out by settlers and conquistadors. Later in his life, Las Casas (1997) wrote a philosophical defense of indigenous peoples which is still read to this day.

Recall Aristotle's description of the "natural slave": one who could not use their reason toward deliberative ends. And remember the importance of reason to philosophers such as Kant in their attempt to racially divide properly human beings from not-properly human beings. Well, Las Casas argued that the "Indios" – the indigenous peoples of the Americas – did not at all lack an ability to use reason, as many of the Spanish conquistadors believed. Moreover, Las Casas pointed out that, even if they did not know Christ, the Indios still exhibited collective virtues lacking in the Christian conquistadors. His point was that the Indios were eminently equipped with the rationality and moral character to receive Christ and become good Christians.

Why are we starting with Las Casas? Here's the thing with comparative politics: you can only identify differences if you imagine the units that you're comparing to be in some way, shape, or fashion, similar. Utterly different entities can't be compared. In defending the Indios, Las Casas also sought out commonality. He accepted that it was no fault of the Indios that they had never heard the good news of the Gospel. It didn't matter what religion you belonged to or where you lived, what really mattered was whether you could use your (God-given) reason to govern your people in a virtuous manner. Nonetheless, the corollary to this logic was that if you did not accept Christianity when it was presented to you then you were obviously not reasonable nor virtuous. This, in fact, was exactly the justification used by Spanish Conquistadors to enslave indigenous people and dispossess them of their lands.

Perhaps you can catch the paradox in Las Casas's defense of the Indios. He accepted that cultural or religious difference was a reality of the human experience: all human groups valued their lives and lived them in different ways. What ultimately made humans human was the basic capacity of each group to use their reason to govern themselves in a virtuous and orderly fashion. But for Las Casas the Christian order was doubtless the most virtuous and orderly. Ultimately, then, he evaluated difference for the purpose of assessing the ability of each human group to assimilate into the universal order of Christendom through its imperial arm – the Spanish empire.

This is what I called in the Introduction the "colonial paradox of comparison." The seemingly paradoxical logic is that, on the one hand, difference is accepted analytically – meaning, how we understand our human experience by breaking it down into logically connecting parts, while on the other hand, difference is disavowed normatively – meaning, how we believe that we *should* live as humans (see in general Inayatullah and Blaney 2004). This paradox is resolved by a colonial project that legitimizes domination and usually violence. This is why in the colonial world the accusation of disorder was almost always laid upon those that resisted assimilation or merely sought to side-step the imposition of (religious or political) values and practices by imperial powers.

We can identify this paradox in many of the philosophers and academics who came after Las Casas. But as we do so we need to grapple with a significant change to the way in which such comparisons were subsequently made. For this purpose, it's necessary to turn to the Scottish enlightenment of the second half of the eighteenth century. There, moral philosophers such as Adam Smith shifted the meaning of virtue from an explicitly religious register based on spiritual belief to a non-religious register based on material "improvement." This shift proved crucial to how we currently conceive of the idea of "development."

The Scots examined the moral significance of "commercial society" – we nowadays call it capitalist society – in a number of ways. One popular strategy was to compare the lives of indigenous peoples in the Americas to those of Europeans (see Blaney and Inayatullah 2010). These comparative inquiries sought out evidence of reason not in religious conversion but in the ability of a group to "improve" nature to meet their needs (see Bhandar 2018). Virtue, in the eyes of the Scottish philosophers, could be evaluated by the way in which such improvement was a channel for God's grace to be manifested on earth as an increased standard of living – an ever better "good life."

In 1767 Adam Ferguson, one of those Scots, wrote an *Essay on the History of Civil Society*. For Ferguson (1995, 35), the "principal spring of human actions" was the "care of subsistence," meaning, the ability to use reason to improve one's surrounding environment. Ferguson (1995, 12) argued that this capacity for "improvement" was evident across humanity and could be found "through the streets of the populous city, or the wilds of the forest." Note here, as with Las Casas, the claim to a common humanity, albeit now made with a materialistic rather than religious logic.

On the one hand, then, Ferguson was what we would nowadays call a "cultural relativist": someone who believes that there is no universal standard by which one can morally evaluate the practices and values of different groups. For Ferguson, so long as each group demonstrated some kind of rational ability to improve nature to meet their needs then how they did so – and how successfully they did so – could have no moral significance.

On the other hand, Ferguson presented what we would nowadays call a "developmental" narrative. The better that humanity could improve their living standard, the more they channeled God's grace on earth. Crucially, Ferguson believed that developing the capacity to improve nature also developed that group's capacity to reason:

> What the savage projects, or observes, in the forest, are the steps which led nations, more advanced, from the architecture of the cottage to that of the palace, and conducted the human mind from the perceptions of sense, to the general conclusions of science. (Ferguson 1995, 14)

Contrast the provincial and limited "perception of sense" – what you know is only what you immediately feel – to the universal and expansive "conclusions of science" – what you feel can be generalized to explain all the phenomena of the world. There is a sense, here, that one path of improvement is definitely more superior (and efficacious) than others: the path forged by Europeans in the making of commercial society.

Ferguson argued that the generalization of knowledge, which enabled a superior kind of improvement, required a specific division of labor. Within this division, each individual had to perform a different task whether that be farming, science, or philosophizing etc. That meant that no one individual could provide all the needs of their subsistence; each was dependent on the work of the other. This interdependency of needs was met through the market mechanism: we all come with different things to sell, and the principles of demand and supply assure the satiation of our needs without recourse to stealing etc. For Ferguson, as for so many of the Scottish philosophers, commercial society had a pacifying and civilizing effect on a divided and wretched humanity.

Here's that colonial paradox at work again, right? Ferguson typified the human condition as the use of reason to improve nature. He accepted that different human groups would improve their surroundings in different ways. The type of improvement was not morally significant neither was its efficacy, only the fact that humans undertook improvement. At the same time, though, Ferguson identified a particular path of improvement through which God's grace was amplified and channeled. That path was taken by Europeans who used their reason to evolve commercial society.

With Las Casas we saw that a seeming paradox of comparison was resolved with a project of religious conversion and conquest. What project did Ferguson propose to resolve the paradox? To be honest, he never directly told us, although it is possible to infer his driving interest from the context within which he wrote his history of civil society as a subject of Britain.

Britain was a polity formed in 1707 by two countries, England and Scotland, both of which harbored colonial aspirations. Ferguson's life spanned the high point of Britain's first empire, comprised of Ireland and the North American and Caribbean colonies. More importantly, he wrote his *Essay* against the backdrop of a world war (the Seven Years War 1756–1763) between the British and French, wherein indigenous peoples were on both sides in the conflicts that took place in the north east of the American continent. While Ferguson's political position on the War focused on the desirability of creating militias in Scotland to defend against a possible French invasion, I want to suggest that this national zeal also shaped his discussion on the improvement of indigenous peoples.

Ferguson seems to have been concerned both for the loyalty of indigenous peoples to the British and the possibility of their radicalization against the British by the French. Ferguson chided those who might wish to accelerate the development of the indigenous peoples of the Americas; and he also disapproved of those who wished to suspend development altogether. Walking the fine line between keeping indigenous peoples on the side of the British, but on the terms of the British, Ferguson (1995, 12) reminded his audience that improvement, for the most part, was not made through "rapid and hasty transitions" but rather through "progressive and slow" steps. Neither revolution nor stasis but orderly and tutored progress was Ferguson's ideal image of improvement. Tutored by the British, of course, as part of a slow process of assimilation.

Let's move on now to the next context wherein the colonial paradox of comparison shifted once more, this time by reference to the challenges of what came to be known as "colonial development." With the loss of some of its American colonies and then in the aftermath of the abolition of slavery, Britain expanded and deepened its dominion across South Asia and Africa. By the late nineteenth century, the empire reached its maximum extent, covering one third of the earth's surface. This expansion was accompanied by increased competition between other European empires and the USA. Competition made the British government concerned for the empire's "undeveloped estates" – those hinterland areas that colonial administration had yet to sufficiently exploit by "improving" nature and profiting from it. At this point, Ferguson's concern over the orderly improvement of "natives" returned, but in new form.

After World War I, Lord Lugard (1922) presented the famous idea that colonial rule was comprised of a "dual mandate" to strengthen empire economically while simultaneously enhancing the social and intellectual capacities of the "native." In 1929, British parliament passed the first Colonial Development Act. With this, "development" now replaced the notion of "improvement."

In the two decades that followed, development projects focused exclusively on the capacity to extract resources. In contrast, anthropologists concerned themselves with the other mandate proposed by Lugard: the effect of colonial development on the "native"; and none more so than the most influential anthropologist of the inter-war years, Bronislaw Malinowski. In his work on the Western Pacific, Malinowski pioneered a new approach to the study of native culture, which went far beyond the "arm chair" mode of speculation that had been convention for much of the nineteenth century. Malinowski advocated for language learning and long-term co-occupation with the native research subject in their sites of habitation.

From his significant experience in the "field," and like Las Casas and Ferguson before him, Malinowski held to the premise that natives and Europeans shared common features of humanity, especially the ability to reason. In Malinowski's (1954, 17) estimation, all cultures around the world demonstrated the existence of a basic "scientific attitude." Yet Malinowski also shared with Ferguson the assumption that a mere potential for this attitude did not mean that "savage" cultures could independently develop themselves into the advanced civilizations found in Europe. Natives remained constrained by a simple and local mindset; European culture activated the scientific outlook in dynamic and universalizing ways.

However, a far more salient issue for Malinowski lay in the fact that colonial development was eroding the very basis for such comparisons between natives and Europeans. What happened, he asked, when European practices started to intimately impress themselves upon native culture? This pressure was nowhere more pronounced than in the settler colonies on the African continent – Kenya, North and South Rhodesia, and South Africa. There, white settlements bordered native lands.

The development of significant extractive industries such as mining created new townships wherein white and black – settlers and natives – met and worked. In the last chapter we encountered the fear that industrial urbanization in Britain and North America might degenerate the Anglo-Saxon race. By the inter-war years this fear had migrated to the colonies. The urbanization of natives caused by colonial development particularly troubled Malinowski.

Recall Ferguson's concern for an orderly pace to indigenous change. Political order in African colonies usually depended upon a system first practiced by the British in late-eighteenth-century Bengal. With so-called "indirect rule," European administrators selected and supported local "chiefs" to rule rural areas on their behalf. Malinowski drew attention to the "deep seated moral and legal force behind such native sanction," which made "a law-abiding citizen out of a so called savage." He worried that this sanction would be undermined by the disorder of urbanization:

the truth that you cannot with impunity undo or subvert an old system of traditions, of morals or laws and replace it by a ready-made new morality and sense of right; the result invariably will be what might be "black bolshevism [communism]." (Malinowski 1929, 28)

We'll come across this association of native-led development with communism presently. For the moment, let's work through Malinowski's assertion that a new kind of African was being created in the urban areas. As he entered into European schools or work places (and for Malinowski it was always a "he"), the native would experience the "overwhelming" superiority of European ways and seek out a Western education so as to acculturate himself to the colonizer's norms and values. But upon returning to his colony, the native would come up against a "color bar" wherein specific occupations were reserved for Europeans only.

Malinowski was most concerned with the reaction of the native to the rejection of his ambition to assimilate to European norms and values. Having already been detribalized, this educated native would create movements modelled on European politics, but ones, Malinowski suggested, that were infected with race hatred. Through mutated movements such as black nationalism the urban native – now a native "elite" – would pursue his revenge upon the British Empire by agitating for political independence.

In seeking to ensure "normal and stable [native] development" and thereby avoid "dangerous consequences" for Britain's empire, Malinowski then gave a stunning prescription. Instead of advocating for a removal of the color bar in administrative occupations, he advised the opposite. Colonial administrators needed to stop preaching to Africans "that a 'full identity' with civilization can ever be reached by them" (Malinowski 1945, 161). In short, natives needed to stay in their place.

Malinowski was adamant that despite their potential to think rationally and with a "scientific outlook," natives could not actualize this potential without European tutorship.

By this reasoning, an independence of political opinion among native elites could in no way be taken as a sign of reasonable adaption to a new environment. Instead, Malinowski presumed that the native would only be able to react with resentment and revenge. This is why Malinowski was adamant that native elites should not be promised an assimilation that the racist division of colonial labor would never allow, because that refusal would create disorder.

Comparison presumes commonality. But what if your claim of commonality required the assimilation of others? And what if those others wanted to pursue different lines of development? Then you would judge their difference to be disorderly. Those who could not assimilate would have to be contained and segregated. For the sake of imperial order, Malinowski ultimately prescribed the later. In 1948, South Africa formally began apartheid.

We might say, then, that the decline of the British Empire made Malinowski resolve the age-old paradox of colonial comparison by giving up on its humanistic propositions, i.e. accepting immutable and hierarchical differences between races. But just as British imperial power declined, American military power rose. Scholars in the US academy rejuvenated the paradox of comparison, this time as part of a putatively impartial science of political development.

Political Development and the Committee on Comparative Politics

The end of World War II was followed by a new Cold War. You've probably read about two systems vying for global supremacy – capitalism versus communism – and represented by two power-blocs – the West versus the East. But there was another axis to the Cold War. At the end of World War II, British, French and Dutch empires began the process of formal decolonization. Crucially, the prospect of winning the Cold War was in part determined by which power block would win over the newly independent polities. The Cold War era thus triangulated struggles between the West, East and South: capitalism versus communism, as well as colonial dependence versus independence (Saull 2005). This was the geopolitical context in which comparative politics became formalized as a subfield of political science.

By the start of World War II, social scientists were already mobilizing to serve the national security interests of the US. In 1939, the Council on Foreign Relations began a War and Peace studies program with the aiming of bringing academics and diplomats into conversation. The Office of Strategic Services, a forerunner of the CIA, also brought in many famous scholars to serve in their Research and Analysis Branch. Academic organizations, such as the Social Science Research Council (SSRC), increasingly grappled with the new landscape of US geopolitical interests.

In 1943 the Committee on World Regions of the SSRC wrote an internal report. Acknowledging the "lack" of knowledge of geographical regions that the war had "focused attention on," the Committee forecast that, after victory, the United States would "enjoy unexampled opportunities and face heavy responsibilities" (Wallerstein 1997, 195–196). The report also suggested that, to address these opportunities and responsibilities, the US academy would require a careful study of the ways in which the general theories of human behavior might or might not apply to different social and geographical contexts. The report's authors looked toward the "comparative method" as a useful tool for pursuing these academic responsibilities that would come with US global leadership. In 1953, the SSRC set up a new Committee on Comparative Politics (CCP). The two lead academics, Pendleton Herring and Gabriel Almond were both behavioralists.

In the last chapter I connected the rise of behavioralism to the science of race heredity. The political question at stake in behaviorism was whether different kinds of peoples – indigenous, black peoples, Mexicans, Jews, East European immigrants – were capable of being trained up to act as responsible and orderly citizens of a democratic society. While behaviorism of this sort was obsessed with the domestic mix of peoples, the scholars associated with the CCP wished to "scale up" behavioral analysis so as to address an international mix of polities. By shifting analysis in this way, CCP scholars could address some urgent questions: how different were the systems of these newly independent societies, and were these differences a barrier to their orderly development toward the Western block? (see Engerman 2010)

CCP scholars began by establishing some functional prerequisites of a society. First and foremost, the "political system" of a society had to produce a harmony rather than conflict of purpose. Conflict over competing interests was to be mitigated by a separation of powers across a set of bureaucratic offices, all of which had discrete and clearly defined roles to play. Harmony would be ensured by shared goals and shared normative regulation of the means to attain those goals. Clear sanctions for disruptive forms of behavior would guarantee a "certain stability" or "changing equilibrium" (Aberle et al. 1950; Almond 1956, 393).

Secondly, it followed that, in order to be harmonious, a society had to be an endogenous unit. This did not mean that a society had to be fully self-sufficient in every material resource that it needed – food, minerals etc. Rather, "endogeneity" pertained to the way in which a functional bureaucracy should not be dependent on outside forces. In short, a society had to possess a substantively independent political system.

Crucially, both prerequisites had the analytical effect of removing imperial hierarchies and colonial rule from societal comparison. Take the first one: harmony. By this measure, the US could hardly be a society if its native peoples still struggled for and claimed the right to self-governance. Notably, in one of the key academic papers that laid out the two prerequisites, the authors dismissed the prospect that "American Indians" could in any way be defined as an "independent entity" (Aberle et al. 1950, 102). (Just to be clear, the US Constitution itself considers those indigenous groups who made treaties with the government to be sovereign.) The point is that by holding to the expectation of harmony, it was impossible to consider that the US was still a settler-colony in conflict.

Now take the second prerequisite: endogeneity. To hold to this expectation meant that none of the societies that you might offer up for comparison could be dependent upon and/ or part of imperial hierarchies. Just think for a moment of the analytical ramifications. Say you wanted to compare the differences between political systems in an era of decoloniz-ation, an era where the majority of states that presently occupy the UN came into being out of colonies. Now imagine that your analytical framework was so constricted that all it could see was independent polities magically appearing out of thin air!

Here's the key point: the prerequisites of harmony and endogeneity required a comparative framework of analysis that elided the fact that the majority of societies in the world had been – and were still being – shaped by struggles over colonial rule and imperial order. But that couldn't erase the fact that the political systems of these newly independent polities were quite different to Western systems. So how did CCP scholars account for the difference without directly and substantively analyzing struggles over colonialism and empire?

They did so by turning to an ideal type method of analysis, first authored by the late-nineteenth-century German sociologist Max Weber. Although Weber's use of the term was quite complex and convoluted, by "ideal type" most social scientists simply mean a set of key features that are present in any particular manifestation of the same phenomenon. Ideal types are meant to be snapshots of a system rather than explanations for how these systems have come into being.

It was in principle possible for CCP scholars to come up with ideal types of social and political struggle. But these might nullify the functional prerequisites of society, which they had ascribed to in the building of their comparative framework. Instead, then, a number of typologies were proffered all of which presented a binary set of ideal types. By binary, I mean logical opposites to each other such as "non-industrialized versus industrialized" or "under-developed versus developed." The most influential typology, however, was associated with the narrative of "modernization" (see especially Gilman 2007; Bhambra 2007). At the 1959 CCP conference, Edward Shils (1910–1995), a sociologist influenced by Max Weber, proposed that all societies could be categorized as either "modern" or "traditional." The modernization narrative accepted that societies could radically change over time. But Shils framed comparative analysis not in terms of a struggle over change but via a snapshot taken of a society before and after transformation.

Shils (1960) defined the ideal typical features of modern political systems as comprising of: democracy, equalitarianism, reformism, universalism in terms of rights and citizenship, a scientific outlook, industrialization, and national sovereignty (Shils 1960, 266). Shils also argued that, despite being ideologically "anti-Western," the Soviet Union and communist China displayed elements of modernity (e.g. scientific outlook, industrialization). In this regard, the East, for Shils, seemed to be pursuing a degenerative modernization. However, in distinct contrast to both West and East power blocs lay the "Asian and African states." Most of these states had entrenched "traditional" political systems, the ideal typical features of which Shils listed as kinship, caste, and local loyalties all of which bred "particularistic spirit" and "parochial loyalties" ill-suited to the universalism and scientific outlook of modern systems.

Now, recall the colonial paradox of comparison: analytical acceptance of difference, normative disavowal of difference. The paradox arose, I have suggested, from a claim that among the diversity of human experience and behavior one could still find commonalities. Las Casas pointed to reason and virtue; Ferguson pointed to the "improvement" of nature; even Malinowski, at least before he advocated racial segregation, admitted a shared mental capacity to develop the scientific outlook. For his part, Shils identified commonalities in the fact that all societies were capable of becoming modern. He acknowledged that modern societies had a particular geographical origin in Western civilization. But he also proposed that "modernity" was a condition that could be "detached in some way from its geographical origins and locus."

This proposition created a different kind of paradox for CCP scholars. It's important to identify this uniqueness so that we can reconceptualize the meaning of "political development" for comparative analysis. Las Casas, Ferguson, and Malinowski all sought to resolve the paradox by reference to the growth or preservation of empire: Spanish conquest, British colonization, and British imperial decline, respectively. But by proposing a common capacity to modernize, and then analyzing difference via snapshots, that is, ideal typical features of "modern" and "traditional" societies, CCP scholars implied that modernization was a process detached from the political interests of any imperial design (Blaney and Inayatullah 2002, 108–112).

In a sense, this detachment reflected the nature of the US as a post-war great power. Yes, it had undertaken imperial expansion at the end of the nineteenth century; but it had not risen to leadership of the "Free World" in the aftermath of World War II by way of expanding its imperium. For the first decades of the Cold War the US represented itself to the decolonizing world as a fellow polity created by a founding act of anti-colonial self-determination (against the British). And to be fair, CCP scholars never normatively endorsed the US as the most virtuous of all political systems.

Yet they did in a surreptitious or indirect way. Because CCP scholars assumed the US to be the *exemplary* modern society. To be clear, this was an analytical rather than normative claim: the US was that society which most closely displayed all the ideal-types associated with the "modern" condition. Actually, for the most part, the ideal typical features of modern society had been extracted by CCP scholars from the particulars of the US political system itself, especially the use of bureaucratic offices to harmoniously balance interests (see for example Almond 1956). CCP scholars also made it abundantly clear that the USSR was a degenerative type of modern society when compared to the US. Above all, they considered the rationality of Asian and African elites to be suspect and to be in danger of following the wrong path to modernization, ending up in the communist bloc.

Now we can bring the strands of the argument together. CCP scholars presented the US as the purest case of modernization. While this presumption was expressed in analytical terms – the way in which a phenomenon is studied – it was, nonetheless, closely attached to a normative preference – a claim that all other paths of modernization were degenerative compared to the US trajectory. And remember: the CCP had skin in the game. Funded, in part, to clarify national security interests, the CCP project was institutionally connected to the Cold War struggle between two power blocs struggling to shape the global order through different organizing principles (capitalist or communist). Ultimately, the modernization narrative was used to legitimize bloody counter-insurgency programs launched by the US state to destabilize regimes that in their opinion were tacking too closely toward the East (see Latham 2010).

I would not want to describe all CCP scholars as stooges of what would come to be called neo-imperialism – the use of military and economic power not to conquer and hold territory but to reshape governments and direct their policy-making processes. That said though, CCP scholars mobilized some of the same logics of comparison as those intellectuals who had defended past imperial powers. Above all, these logics are evident in the normative assumption that decolonization might create social disorder.

I suspect that when it came to evaluating order and disorder on a global level, CCP scholars were in part influenced by pre-war domestic debates over citizenship. You'll remember from the last chapter that debates over political behavior pivoted on a racial logic that distinguished competent and incompetent citizens via the ascription of normal and abnormal political behavior. On top of this established influence, CCP scholars picked up key insights directly from Malinowski and other anthropologists in terms of identifying the breakdown of norms and values that came with urbanization and colonial development.

All of these influences and insights were parsed through the ideal types associated with modernization. Shils, for instance, shared much of Malinowski's analysis of those natives who had partially left their traditional societies and ventured into the European urban areas. Due to their education, Shils proposed, native elites believed in the "truth of science" rather than the traditional "wisdom of tribal elders." Yet Shils was suspicious of the modernity of native elites: they were only "somewhat detribalized" and "less completely than they themselves often think" (Shils 1960, 273). Straddling, perforce, the traditional and the modern bred reactionary tendencies in native elites rather than rational prescriptions.

Shils described these tendencies in a narrative of mutation and degeneration, which was once again extremely close to Malinowski's. Measuring themselves by the West's yardsticks, but identifying themselves with their non-Western compatriots, native elites were overly sensitive to the relative impoverishment of their societies vis-à-vis Europe and even the US. While praising the "wisdom of the simple and the humble" folk who had suffered colonialism, native elites still distrusted the masses whom they deemed to be too "traditional." In the inter-war context, Malinowski had feared "black bolshevism." In the Cold War context, Shils worried that native elites would shun the orderly guidance of the exemplary modern US, embrace socialism, align to the Eastern bloc, and craft "extremist [populist] solutions."

To summarize the argument so far. CCP scholars fixed their comparative analysis on the ideal types found in the modernization narrative: traditional versus modern. The features of these ideal types did not directly reference struggles over imperial rule and colonization but presented snapshots of a "before' and "after." Yet when it came to decolonization, CCP scholars nonetheless used particular colonial logics to adjudicate the development paths of native elites by reference to an exemplary path of modernization, a path that led to capitalism (and the US) rather than communism (and the USSR).

Therefore, while CCP scholars were realistic enough to point out diverging paths of development, they held to an underlying support for assimilation, or at least, a preferential alignment of decolonizing societies into the US-led bloc of Cold War politics. That was how they resolved the paradox of comparison: by presuming that the only non-degenerative path of modernization led to the US. This, I would suggest, is the key to reconceptualizing the concept of "political development." And in these ways, the colonial paradox of comparison was formative to the emergence of comparative politics as a subfield of political science.

I've given you a quite dense argument. So, for clarity's sake, let's look at it in action with the work of Lucian Pye (1921–2008). A little background. Pye undertook his first fieldwork in colonial Malaya between 1952 and 1953. At this point in time, the British colony was under a state of emergency due to a deadly guerilla war fought between British Commonwealth forces and the armed wing of the Malayan Communist Party. Therefore Pye's fieldwork was undertaken in the cauldron of Cold War politics where an eastward-facing radicalization of colonial populations seemed to be manifesting. In 1963, Pye succeeded Gabriel Almond as the chairperson of CCP.

Pye typified non-Western societies as "traditional" ones, wherein personalities, prestige, and communal affiliations created power struggles to the detriment of impartial, rational policy making. Similarly, Pye was keen to mark off the cultural distinction between the masses and elite intellectuals who had been urbanized and educated along Western lines. These intellectuals often faced off against older generations of traditional rulers. Drawing upon the ideal types associated with the modernization narrative, Pye (1958) presented non-Western societies as prone to violence, instability, and fracture, and he made sense of such disorders by focusing on the ideas and actions of native elites.

But Pye was no ideologue. And he was extremely sensitive to the presumption that the US represented the normative endpoint of human evolution. He noted that in political discourse the concept of "development" had now taken the place of older concepts such as "improvement" or "progress." In search of a science of political behavior, Pye (1965, 2–3) admitted that many academics were "embarrassed" by the almost religious faith that they had previously invested in the triumph of the Western way. And the Shoah (Jewish holocaust), Pye added, had injected a definite mood of agnosticism and skepticism over this article of faith.

Furthermore, Pye cautioned against a full embrace of "cultural relativism." He understandably feared that such relativism might work to naturalize the empirical fact that some societies were rich and some poor. This naturalization, argued Pye, led to a static mode of analysis wherein the changing nature of politics within and across societies could not be accounted for.

In fine, Pye sought out a middle-ground from which to define "political development" in a "scientific" manner – a manner that took the fact of development seriously but shunned any ideological claims about where development should lead. For this purpose, Pye critically took apart and evaluated common assumptions about political development even among Western academics. This procedure actually led him to question the two functional prerequisites of a society originally endorsed by CCP scholars: harmony and endogeneity.

When it came to a lack of harmony of purpose, Pye directly alluded to colonial legacies in non-Western political systems, especially the introduction of "rationalized institutions of administration" set apart from the majority of the people. These colonial legacies, Pye (1965, 9) admitted, explained to some extent why non-Western states were confronted with the "classic issue of balancing popular sentiments with public order." Pye also questioned the premise of endogeneity. Political development, he pointed out, took place:

> within a historical context in which influences from outside the society impinge on the process of social change just as change in the different aspects of a society – the economy, the polity and social order – all impinge on each other. (Pye 1965, 11)

This was a remarkable admission. Remember that the expectation of societal harmony and political endogeneity had elided any framing of comparison through struggles over colonial rule. Instead, comparison was framed by two snapshots of change, before and after – the ideal types of traditional and modern society. By eschewing the expectation of harmony and endogeneity, Pye's critique threatened to replace the modernization narrative with a focus on unequal relations in a world system, an idea to which we will presently turn.

Pye finished his appraisal of the concept of political development by establishing three themes that the CCP would henceforth use as their comparative framework of analysis. But guess what: all three supported the strategy of explaining difference via traditional and modern ideal types! What's more, these themes effectively set the modern features of equality, scientific outlook and universalism as the key measures for evaluating the success of political development. In contrast, Pye presented traditional features of patronage, irrational belief, and provinciality as signs of degeneracy and disorder especially when mobilized by native elites for the purposes of development.

Indeed, while he alluded to them in the course of his critical inquiry, colonial entanglements and imperial legacies did not feature at all in Pye's ultimate framing of comparison between traditional and modern political systems. Instead, he suggested that any differences between societies could be explained simply by the sequence in which discrete political systems engaged with putting in place equality, a scientific outlook, and universalism. In other words, different sequences within a societal process of modernization accounted for different paths of political development. Struggle over imperial order and colonial rule vanished from his comparative framework of analysis.

Pye's torturous argument demonstrates how CCP scholars re-asserted the colonial paradox of comparison even as they sought to instigate a comparative analysis absent of colonially induced terminology. All political systems had the potential to modernize. Modernization invoked neither a colonial logic nor an imperial interest. Nonetheless, paths of modernization were adjudicated according to their degeneration from an ideal type of modern polity which was exemplified by the US. The project that immediately drove this adjudication pertained to West and East power blocs struggling to craft a capitalist or communist global order. Crucially, the degeneration of non-Western polities was explained through the old colonial logics that feared the disorderly independence pursued by native elites. Except that these potential disorders now referenced a struggle between capitalist and communist blocs rather than the integrity of one empire.

The CCP project could never acknowledge just how fundamental colonial logics were to its analysis, even in the era of decolonization. There were, though, other scholarly communities in the world aside from the CCP. Some of them sought to make sense of political development by direct reference to the uneven global relations that empire and capitalism had generated and which still existed, albeit in new iterations. One of these scholarly communities at Dar es Salaam University allows us to reimagine development as under-development.

Under-Development and Dar es Salaam University

In 1966 a military coup in Ghana overthrew Kwame Nkrumah, one of the most famous independence leaders in the post-World-War-II era of decolonization. Subsequently, the revolutionary center of the African continent shifted to the east. Tanzania had achieved independence in 1961 under Julius Nyerere, head of the Tanganyika African National Union (TANU). Although educated at Edinburgh university, Nyerere was an advocate of "African socialism." In his estimation, socialism was not just a European invention but had indigenous roots in African principles of democratic communalism. Nyerere's ideology attracted to Tanzania's capital city, Dar es Salaam, a host of famous revolutionary figures: Che Guevara, Malcolm X, and Angela Davis to name a few.

Nyerere was precisely the kind of native elite that scholars such as Malinowski, Shils, and Pye feared. From the beginning of independence, Nyerere promoted an ethic of self-help to redress the legacies of colonial dependency. In February 1967, he issued the Arusha Declaration that bound the development of Tanzania to three principles: self-reliance (through the mobilization of domestic human and capital resources); social equity (by disbursing benefits from the rich to the poor and especially from the urban to the rural); and cooperative effort (via the collectivization of economic activities, especially farming).

Education featured heavily in a corollary to the Arusha Declaration. There, the system inherited from colonialism was indicted for providing no instruction in collective self-reliance. Colonial rule had soured school pupils toward rural life while sweetening the prospect of joining the urban bureaucratic administration. Nyerere himself directed this critique toward higher education: "we in poor societies can only justify expenditure on a university, of any type, if it promotes real development of our people" (Coleman 1986, 478).

The colonial system of higher education in British East Africa began in 1949, when Makerere College, in the British protectorate of Uganda, entered into an arrangement with the University of London to become one of its colleges. The University College of East Africa grew to encompass several institutions across the region. In the year of Tanzanian independence, one of those institutions opened in Dar es Salaam.

By the time of the Arusha Declaration, the college at Dar es Salaam was patched together by a set of tensions. Firstly, in 1964 its campus was relocated to a hill eight miles away from the city center and government administration. Secondly, the college's administrative structures were nevertheless increasingly controlled by Nyerere's party, TANU. Thirdly, degrees were still conferred by the University of London, in the capital of the old imperial center. Triangulate these tensions and you come up with the following tensions that ran through the college: an educational space apart from politics versus a vehicle for politicians, and a space for post-colonial self-reliance versus an avatar of old imperial dependence (see Shivji 1993).

Very shortly after the Arusha Declaration a conference was organized on the "Role of the University College, Dar Es Salam, in a Socialist Tanzania." The conference discussed what we nowadays call "decolonizing the curriculum" (see Bhambra, Gebrial, and Nişancıoğlu 2018; Chantiluke, Kwoba, and Nkopo 2018). Some scholars advocated for a curricular emphasis on Tanzanian and East African politics and history, and an embedding of academic learning in (especially rural) community service. Nine college lecturers strongly promoted such changes, but specifically to help develop "an indigenous Tanzanian socialism, with an international outlook" ("Draft Recommendations of the Conference on the Role of the University College, Dar es Salaam, in a Socialist Tanzania" 1967, 562).

Actually, none of the left-leaning "group of nine" was Tanzanian. Most of them had been recruited from outside the African continent. As they arrived in independent Tanzania the "group of nine" confronted the modernization narrative that informed the World Bank's first five-year plan for the country, and which other visiting academics from the West subscribed to (Campbell 1991). This narrative proposed that the internal dynamics of Tanzanian society were lacking in many of the ideal typical features of a modern society, and that development comprised largely of introducing these features through external assistance rather than, as Nyerere intended, from internal self-reliance.

We are now going to interrogate the work of three of the most prominent radical scholars at Dar es Salaam, all of whom refuted the policy prescriptions arising out of a modernization approach. Their scholarship instead presented development as part of a global system of capitalist accumulation that was structured through imperial legacies and neo-imperial impulses.

In 1965, John Saul, a Canadian political scientist, arrived in Tanzania to undertake his PhD fieldwork on rural development. The following year he arranged a contract to teach at Dar es Salaam through Canada's External Aid agency

(Saul 2010, 24). Subsequently, Saul became involved in the Mozambique struggle for liberation from Portuguese rule. Giovanni Arrighi (2009), an Italian economist, arrived in Tanzania one year after Saul. He had come directly from the University College of Rhodesia and Nyasaland – now University of Zimbabwe. As a lecturer there, Arrighi had participated in the Rhodesian (Zimbabwean) liberation struggle and was thrown out for his anti-colonial activities. Walter Rodney, a Guyanese historian, arrived in Dar es Salaam in 1967 by way of London. After finishing a PhD at SOAS, he was given a Tanzanian placement by the British Ministry of Overseas Development. Rodney would become the preeminent Caribbean activist-intellectual of the Black Power era. In 1980, he was assassinated in Guyana by the Burnham regime.

I mentioned in the last chapter that after World War II, and with the onset of the Cold War, US scholars worried that the label "social science" might imply an association with socialism. Better, then, to use the term "behavioralist science," which could connotate neutrality and objectivity rather than bias and ideology. Recall also that CCP scholars such as Pye believed that their use of ideal types inoculated them against charges of ideological distortion of the facts. Ok, now remember that for CCP scholars the ideal type features of a modern society included a "scientific outlook" instead of traditional myths and rituals. It was precisely this inability to fully embrace the scientific outlook that made the likes of Malinowski, Shils, and Pye suspicious of the political careers of native elites. Put all these things together, and it becomes clear that claiming your academic work as "scientific" was never just a description but unavoidably a political act.

Rodney, Arrighi, and Saul were also committed to a scientific outlook on development. Their "scientific socialism" decried the idea of "neutrality" as a cover used by powerful interests in the production of knowledge. All three scholars clearly identified the universities of newly independent African polities as sites complicit in colonial rule, and wherein intellectual struggles over the practice of "science" would in part determine the path of political development. Let's now turn to the arguments they made while at Dar es Salaam.

It's useful to begin with Rodney (1968) because his work, at this time, directly implicates education in the politics of colonial rule. Rodney notes that Tanzanian independence has led to an expansion of the "modern sector of the economy" – typified by buying and selling for the accumulation of capital – in distinction to the "traditional" activities – typified by subsistence farming. Independence, in Rodney's estimation, has therefore increased demands for productivity (so as to accumulate more capital), capital equipment (to enable such productivity), foreign skills (including teachers such as Rodney), and the importation of more consumer goods (for those who now had more disposable income).

The problem, notes Rodney, is that in all these matters – in technology, money markets, and purchasing parity – the former imperial centers retain all the power. In short, with independence "imperialist domination" continues in a "new guise." Crucially, this neo-imperialism – the persistence of economic dependence even after political independence – is as much a project of new national elites as it is of old imperial powers. And here's where education comes into the picture.

Rodney explains how the colonial schooling system that Tanzania inherits upon independence is designed to support "economic exploitation, social inferiority, and political dependence" (Rodney 1968, 71). Due to the color bars of colonial rule, race and education become "correlates" of class. By this Rodney means to say that a distinction obtains between manual and intellectual labor which is at the same time predominantly a distinction between African and non-African workers. Education provides a special path for a few natives to enter into a tiny locally trained bureaucracy that appropriates to itself "a great part of the fruits of the nation's labor" (Rodney 1968, 74). These black elites join "comprador Asians and the white settlers" as "local representatives of the European bourgeoisie" (Rodney 1968, 72).

Now, while these educated Africans protest the racial hierarchies within their elite class – a black phenotype would place you at the bottom of this elite – the kind of change they advocate is equality only *within* the elite. They do not, for instance, advocate mass education and uplift. Yet it is this educated African elite that leads the colonial revolution and wins political independence.

Rodney's analysis shares the ideal type terminology used by CCP scholars, e.g. "traditional" and "modern." He even shares their focus on native elites. But his argument of societal change does not depend at all on the prerequisites upon which CCP scholars frame their comparative analysis. To remind you, these prerequisites are (a) a harmony of purpose, and (b) an endogenous political system. In Rodney's estimation, political independence has not transformed the way in which Tanzania's economy is racially structured along conflicting lines of exclusions and hierarchies inherited from colonialism. Neither has independence done away with the dependency of the ruling class on external forces. This leads Rodney to surmise that native elites are not mutant-modernizers; they are, more accurately, complicit agents in the renewal and reforming of colonial rule and imperial hierarchies.

Arrighi and Saul write a set of papers that share Rodney's aim of situating Tanzanian development within a capitalist global economy built upon imperialism. They, though, ground their analysis in the skewed relations of production in rural areas. Above all, their research demonstrates how imperial hierarchies produce "uneven" development at all levels.

Arrighi and Saul (1968) begin by pointing out that economic development strategy encourages the use of labor outside of the time it takes to provide for a family's subsistence. That is, by using extra labor to produce surplus crops for the market, monies raised might be put to use for innovating agricultural production in general. This development strategy promises to enrich the whole of the rural sector. The catch-22 to this strategy is that it requires significant incentives to be provided in the first place. And these incentives require funding. However, such funds are most likely to have been directed toward the production of "capital goods," meaning machinery that increases productive capacity. Meanwhile, the profits arising from increased productivity are mostly exported out of Tanzania by foreign multinational corporations who tend to invest in capital intensive techniques rather than labor intensive ones.

For these reasons, Arrighi and Saul suggest that increases in productivity never spill over to buoy a wider development of the society across urban and rural divides. By this reasoning they too arrive at Rodney's position: even after formal independence, Tanzania remains dependent on the vagaries of the world market, especially the mercurial demand for primary products.

Arrighi and Saul are adamant that a lack of rural development cannot be adequately explained by strictly national-level factors such as "level of technology." Yet that is exactly the modernization logic that drives the World Bank's five-year plan at independence. CCP scholars attribute Tanzania's development failures to the resentfulness and populism of native elites. Alternatively, Arrighi and Saul argue that whatever capital does remain in the country is captured by the salaries of the elites and then put toward non-productive ends – lifestyle consumption.

For Arrighi and Saul, Tanzania's developmental challenges lie principally in the ways in which the capitalist interests of multinational corporations entwine with the colonial heritage of unequal and segregated labor occupations and salary structures. This kind of "uneven development" reveals the neo-colonial character of global capitalism, which simultaneously produces development for the old imperial powers and under-development for the ex-colonies.

Let me reminisce for a moment. I first visited Nairobi, Kenya, in 1990. At a writer's fair I came across a book that Rodney had written at Dar es Salaam back in 1971 for a non-academic audience. It was the second book written by an academic that I ever bought, although I had dropped out of high school at seventeen and was neither a student nor scholar at the time. I still have that beaten-up copy of *How Europe Underdeveloped Africa*.

Rodney begins his incredibly influential book by describing development in very similar ways to how Ferguson had described improvement – the capacity for a human group to increase their living standard by exploiting the resources of nature. Similar to Ferguson's proposal about the universal propensity for humanity to improve, Rodney declares that all peoples on every continent have historically demonstrated an intellectual and physical aptitude to develop. He makes these universal claims to confound those who believe that only colonial administrators had introduced the modern drive to "develop" into an unthinking African continent.

What's more, Rodney defines development in a way that once again refutes the two prerequisites upon which CCP scholars study societal change: endogeneity and harmony. Firstly, Rodney argues that economic expansion is a universal feature within all societies. But if all societies have been dynamic, then it follows that as societies develop they infringe upon each other, and this infringement becomes part of the development dynamic. In other words, no society has ever really developed endogenously.

Secondly, and consequentially, Rodney asserts that development is fundamentally conflictual. At various points in history, some societies specialize their division of labor to enable more production; but in doing so they exacerbate an inequality in distribution that sparks class conflict. This unevenness also creates a situation whereby societies are "at different levels" when they come into contact with each other. In this case, the economically weaker societies are adversely affected in ways that Rodney and Arrighi and Saul lay out with regard to Tanzania. Hence, conflict and struggle are features of development at every scale of human existence.

Given the fundamentally conflictual and interconnected dynamic of development, Rodney proposes that the concept of "under-development" should not be used to compare so-called traditional and modern societies. Certainly, Rodney admits that the comparison of economic levels of development is a legitimate exercise. But the far more "indispensable" meaning of under-development lies, he claims, in its expression of a "particular relationship of exploitation." In other words, "the exploitation of one country by another" is a "product of capitalist, imperialist and colonialist exploitation" (Rodney

1989, 21–22). Or, in Rodney's famous equation, Europe's development is simultaneously Africa's under-development. Rodney is no idealist. He obviously sees power everywhere. And so, he is careful to acknowledge that socialist countries can also be exploiters. The political question, for Rodney, is not to do with who among the world population are the most virtuous. The question instead is whether "the standard of living in a given industrialized country is a product of its own internal resources or whether it stems from exploiting other countries" (Rodney 1989, 33). Given these dynamics, Rodney argues that "African development is possible only on the basis of a radical break with the international capitalist system, which has been the principal agency of under-development" (Rodney 1989, 7; see also Arrighi and Saul 1968, 151).

Rather than "difference" per se, the radical scholars at Dar es Salaam framed their analysis in terms of globally unequal relations of exploitation that delivered under-development to some and development to others. By focusing on relations of exploitation they managed to avoid the analytical embrace and normative disavowal of difference that comprised the colonial paradox of comparison.

This paradox, and its resolution, always referenced the interests and aims of a dominant power – imperial or neo-imperial. The political stakes of comparison involved the claim that one path of development was considered the most virtuous one, by clear statement or by implication. Entangled with the scholarly pursuit of comparison was a stark geopolitical choice: assimilate or be militarily/fiscally disciplined. Dar es Salaam scholars invested themselves in another set of political stakes: redressing the inequities of exploitation by struggling at all levels against neo-imperial capitalism.

Conclusion

The comparative framework that CCP scholars initiated did not stay uncontested for long. By the early 1970s, there was widespread dissatisfaction with one of its underlying premises, namely that political systems functioned harmoniously. After a decade of military coups and a decline in democratic practices across much of the newly independent states, comparativists turned toward theories that could better explain conflict. For this purpose, scholars stepped back from the grand yet abstract ideal-types associated with the "modernization" narrative (traditional versus modern) and focused instead on particular institutions in law and government that tangibly constrained and shaped political behaviors.

But the colonial logics present in the formation of comparative politics remain influential in other ways. Recall that with their ideal type method, CCP scholars framed their analysis through binary snapshots – especially traditional/modern. At the same time, though, they mobilized colonially induced logics to evaluate political development. Now, you might shift or shrink the ideal type from, for example, "traditional" to "authoritarian," or "modern" to "democratic," but this in and of itself doesn't mean that you have ejected the colonial logics that lead you to evaluate development paths from one condition to the other.

Take, for instance, the notion of the "failed state." In comparative analysis, no state is ever described as being "successful." Tellingly, the attributes by which one adjudicates "failedness" suspiciously resemble ideal-types gathered from fragments of Western state formation (see Bilgin and Morton 2002). Those states evaluated as failing are mostly post-colonial ones; those that do the evaluating ascribe themselves membership in a successful "international community." Just like the 1950s arguments for modernization, recent arguments for humanitarian intervention have rarely evaluated the imperial and neo-imperial relations that have causally tied the "international community" to failed and failing states in conflictual ways (see Ayoob 2001; Sabaratnam 2016).

More important perhaps is the endurance of the premise of endogeneity. Heloise Weber (2007) points out that the analysis of development – both academic and professional

– remains tied to a "formal comparative method" that elides any analysis of its global constitution beyond state borders. Just think for example of Poverty Reduction Strategy Papers prepared by national administrations as well as the Millennium Development Goals authored by the UN, both of which quantify and evaluate development at a state-by-state level. The premise of endogeneity evaluates mal-development solely at the level of the individual state and government policy. But is there no such thing as an imperial division of labor and a global capitalist system that states are embedded within and constituted through?

I don't want to say that comparativists are ignorant of imperial legacies. That would be extremely unfair. Some scholars have even started to identify a multitude of developmental trajectories that run through the pre-colonial, colonial, and post-colonial histories of specific states (De Juan and Pierskalla 2017). Here lies valuable analysis that recognizes colonialism to be a dynamic force shaping development trajectories during and after the end of formal empire. It is a line of inquiry that Pye gestured toward yet drew back from.

Still, it was this kind of work that Dar es Salaam scholars undertook over forty years ago, especially with regards to Tanzania. And yet Rodney, Arrighi, and Saul did not undertake comparative analysis simply to evaluate differences between polities. They saw the value of their work as reparative. That is, their analysis of under-development served a political and ethical project to re-structure the global order along truly democratic lines such that analysis of and mobilization around inequality, oppression, and violence did not finish at state borders.

The question, then, is whether comparative politics can talk of a politics of reparation without conceding the premises of its comparative method. To address this question, comparativists would need to critically analyze the colonial logics that might be bound to the kind of categories they use to evaluate difference. Remember: even when the categories do not directly reference colonialism, a colonial logic can still operationalize them.

Above all, comparative politics needs to critically assess its commitment to the state as the (endogenous) unit of comparison. If the comparative method cannot pursue these reflections, then I would suggest that it will remain as politically conservative as it was during the days of empire and the era of decolonization. Comparativists should, at least, come to terms with this disposition. One subfield of political science that has conservatively examined global power structures as well as the prospect of global justice is international relations, to which we will now turn.

–5–

International Relations

Throughout this book we've consistently come up against a tension. On the one hand, political theorists, behavioralists, and comparativists have presented the vision of a shared humanity building the "good life" together: democracy, equality, rights, scientific advancements, and so on. On the other hand, these scholars have been circumspect about the capability of all humans to share in this good life equally, if at all. When it comes to the intellectual foundations of political science, a progressive commitment to the good life is never too far removed from a pessimistic outlook on humanity.

Pessimism is the hallmark of the subfield called International Relations (IR). Students inducted into IR will be presented with a fundamental distinction between seeing the world through "realist" or "liberal" lens. A liberal viewpoint aspires to embed the progressive institutions of domestic politics – law, rights, justice, security, peace – within international politics. Realists accuse liberals of idealism in so far as relations between states are already anarchical. In the absence of a world government, realists counter, there can be no law, rights, security, or justice. Therefore, international politics, unlike domestic politics, is prone to war and violence.

For some time, realism was by far the predominant approach in IR. However, since the 1980s scholars have questioned realism's pessimism. The last five decades of globalization, some say, has clearly not proceeded anarchically but with some intentional coherence, even if economic, political, and cultural flows exceed the sovereign control of any one – or group of – states. The structured nature of these flows, scholars have argued, demonstrates the existence of "global governance": a kind of governing that aspires toward a global "good life" even in the absence of one world government (Rosenau and Czempiel 1992). This phenomenon strongly suggests that international politics *can* be regulated in a peaceful manner.

But is the regulation of war and violence a novel pursuit at the global level? Think back, for example, to Las Casas and his fifteenth-century defense of the Indios. What happens if we approach the study of global governance by reference to empire? Robert Vitalis (2015) has recently shown that in the early twentieth-century US academy, those who studied international politics predominantly focused upon relations between empires and their subject peoples. IR began, effectively, as a debate between white and black scholars over the study of imperial governance, the responsibilities of great powers to administrate (separate) "race development" and to thereby avoid "race war" (see Henderson 2017).

Of course, in the early twentieth century the US was not the global power that it became after World War II. In this respect, focus on the US academy needs to be complemented by an inquiry into the British academy which, in the early twentieth century, was most intimately connected to the largest empire in the world. In fact, the subfield of IR formally began in Britain. In 1918 the first chair of International Politics, named after Woodrow Wilson, was endowed at University College of Wales, Aberystwyth. The first named department of "International Relations" began at the London School of Economics in 1927.

In a similar way to colleagues working on the US story, Ian Hall (2015) has uncovered some of the imperial contexts in which IR flourished in the British academy. In this chapter I will build upon Hall's work and argue that the pessimism evident in the study of IR is less a result of the logic of anarchy and more a colonial logic concerning the loss of empire. I will then propose that peace movements in the service of anti-colonial self-determination provide us with a very different logic as to the causes of and prospects for peace on a global level.

In the first part, I will recontextualize the study of international politics by reference to the nineteenth-century "standard of civilization," which legally and morally justified European imperial expansion. I will demonstrate that the principles of equitable inter-dependency between civilized powers and paternalistic dependency for uncivilized peoples jointly underpinned the idea of good imperial governance. By the early twentieth century, many scholars believed that this ideal was manifesting in the British Commonwealth of Nations. I will show that much of the British discussion over "international politics" pertained to the success of the Commonwealth as a replacement for empire.

I will then turn to Martin Wight, an English historian, who in 1959 wrote one of the most famous essays on the difficulties of theorizing international politics in the absence of the "good life" that was secured by domestic politics. Wight is also famous for popularizing the concept of "international society" whose membership comprised diplomats and statesmen intent on limiting the frequency and intensity of war. I will reconceptualize "international society" as none other than the Commonwealth model that Wight admired: inter-dependency for civilized powers, dependency for uncivilized peoples. Wight increasingly associated the worst elements of anarchy – war and violence –with anti-colonial self-determination movements. He longed for the order of empire in an era where colonialism had been normatively and practically undermined by independence movements. That, I will suggest, is the source of his pessimism regarding prospects for peace.

Wight's international society was comprised of elite, mostly white, men. In the last part, I will reimagine the collectives that might pursue peace successfully by taking an "intersectional" approach that renders power in terms of intersecting "axes of oppression." I will use this approach to examine the Nuclear-Free and Independent Pacific movement of the late twentieth century. Led by Pacific women, this peace movement confronted nuclear war, military imperialism, and settler-colonialism as intersecting axes of oppression. Contrary to the colonial logic of Wight's "international society" and his distrust of anti-colonial self-determination, I will propose that the Nuclear-Free and Independent Pacific movement pursued a peace far more salient and fundamental than models of good imperial governance could ever account for.

Good Imperial Governance

You might already have come across the distinction between domestic and international politics, with its corresponding attribution of the good life to the peaceful domestic realm and anarchy to the war-prone international realm. But I want you to think instead about two other interconnected distinctions: firstly, between the inside of an imperium (the areas under imperial domination) and what lies beyond its moving frontiers; and secondly, between civilized powers and uncivilized peoples.

By the nineteenth century a "standard of civilization" was wielded by European powers to regulate and justify imperial expansion (Bowden 2005). European diplomats and politicians ostensibly adjudicated this standard by reference to civic arrangements. For instance, if your polity upheld private property rights, and if (after the 1820s) it outlawed the slave trade, then you could be said to be civilized. If your polity failed to reach this standard, you would be granted the status of "quasi-sovereign," that is, sovereign in principle, but still not civilized enough to exercise that sovereignty competently (Grovogui 1996). In this event you might lose your sovereignty and become, instead, a ward of civilized powers.

A "law of nations" upheld this standard and policed the boundaries between the European "family of nations" and uncivilized others. This boundary affirmed different norms of interaction which correspond to those two distinctions I mentioned above: empire and what lay beyond its borders, and civilized powers versus uncivilized peoples. In the early twentieth century, Lassa Oppenheim, the "father" of modern international law, wrote a treatise that brought these distinctions together through a discussion on "intervention" (see in general Macmillan 2013).

Oppenheim (1920, 1: 233) pointed to the principle of "non-intervention," shared between "all the civilized States as equal members of the Family of Nations." Such a principle did not necessarily outlaw war. And evidently not. But war was deemed to be wrong because it broke the principle. Oppenheim then laid out a series of different rules of engagement between the family of nations and peoples outside of this family. Here, there was no principle of non-intervention. Rather, intervention into other peoples' affairs was permissible under certain circumstances; wars of colonial conquest could even be justified as humanitarian "interventions." The boundary of intervention/non-intervention was slightly porous, occasionally letting some peoples in and occasionally throwing some polities out as "pariahs."

The point is that in Oppenheim's schema, international politics did not take place between the same entities – states – but between qualitatively different entities: civilized powers and non-civilized peoples. What is more, the most powerful of these civilized polities were not states but empires.

You can visualize this international politics in terms of the intersection of two kinds of lines. One line is horizontal and comprised, in principle, of equitable relations between polities. The other lines are all vertical, comprising each empire's hierarchical governing structure. Empires civilized by creating a hierarchical order comprised of the metropolitan society, then self-governing white-settler colonies, and at the bottom, dependencies comprised of non-white, "native" populations. Outside of the family of civilized polities and outside of their empires – beyond the intersecting lines – lay disorder.

Well, the plot thickens. Because Martin Wight grew up in an era where British scholars and administrators had started to think again about their own imperium as a kind of mini-family of nations, comprised of both equitable (horizontal) and hierarchical (vertical) governing structures. This rethinking was given urgency by a crisis of imperial rule that centered upon South Africa.

Recall from the last chapter that by the end of the nineteenth century inter-imperial competition had increasingly put Britain's vast empire under economic and military strain. The stakes were raised further for Britain by the fact that by this time the white settler-colonies of Canada, Australia, New Zealand, and South Africa (the "Dominions") had acquired more and more powers of self-governance. In 1899, a war began between two Boer (Dutch) colonies – the South African Republic and the Orange Free State – and Britain's Cape Colony. The British Empire was so unprepared for the war that it required hundreds of thousands of troops from Australia, New Zealand, and other African colonies to defeat the Boers.

The South Africa War (1899–1902) revealed to Britain's ruling classes that in order to preserve their empire they had better make sure that their white-run and increasingly independent dominions remained a cohesive part of it. This was the moment when an idea for federation, which had first been conceived in the late nineteenth century, became realized in the form of a British Commonwealth of Nations (Bell 2007). From 1921 onwards, the moniker "British Commonwealth" formally replaced that of the "British Empire."

The term "commonwealth" was coined by Jan Smuts, an Afrikaner, participant in the South Africa War, and architect of the Union of South Africa, which, in 1910, united Boer and British colonies. Smuts was also a key advocate of "separate development" – apartheid. He considered black Africans to be morally, socially, and physically immature, and hence a drag upon the advancement of the (now unified) white race in South Africa. Smut's idea for a Commonwealth rested upon a two-tiered family of nations organized along the intersecting lines that I sketched out above. White dominions would enjoy self-governance and be inter-dependent – this is the horizontal line; non-white peoples would be dependent upon white administrators and come under their tutelage – these are the intersecting vertical lines.

By the inter-war years, the Commonwealth had emerged as an institution in which many believed the best hope lay for mitigating war through good imperial governance. The Commonwealth would provide self-governance to those who deserved it and tutelage to those who did not. Some even believed the Commonwealth to be a more effective executor of the League of Nations, in fact, more ideal than the League itself (Mazower 2009, 192). Unlike the League, the Commonwealth could claim to be tightly bound together by a long imperial history, a sharing of (white) populations, and the English language.

The Commonwealth model influenced a generation of scholars interested or involved in international politics. Take, for instance, English-born Lionel Curtis who fought in the South Africa War. Curtis subsequently served as a secretary to Lord Milner, an administrator in South Africa and an influential advocate for imperial reform. Like Smuts, Curtis perceived white unity and self-governance as a crucial requirement if empire was going to ensure that the dependency of immature Africans would not create disorder or degeneration going forward (see Thakur and Vale 2020).

At a meeting with American counterparts during the 1919 Paris peace conference that inaugurated the League of Nations, Curtis mooted the creation of a Royal Institute of International Affairs. The Institute became colloquially known after its location at Chatham House, London. Out of the same conversations arose the US equivalent institute known as the Council on Foreign Relations. Both institutions are still in existence. Anyway, over the next two decades key figures in Chatham House encouraged the establishment of affiliated institutes of international affairs across the British dominions. By the 1930s, Chatham House was increasingly perceiving the challenge of good imperial governance in terms of Commonwealth administration.

Consider, also, Charles Manning, a white South African scholar who, as professor at the London School of Economics, was a mentor to Wight in its Department of International Relations. Manning was convinced that imperialism was the vessel for a "sacred trust of civilization," which provided colonial subjects with tutelage and well-being (Wilson 2004). Manning also envisaged the Commonwealth as an emerging force for this global good. In 1933, at the Preparatory Committee of the first British Commonwealth Relations Conference in Toronto, Manning proposed the formation of the South African Institute of International Affairs.

Once more, though, South Africa posed a significant challenge to the integrity of Britain's imperium. In 1948, the country formally began its apartheid regime – separate (but unequal) development for white, Indian, Asian, "colored," and black races. This racist and inequitable arrangement of self-governance increasingly clashed with a new reality of Commonwealth administration. In the same year, the British Raj gave way to independent India and Pakistan. From here on, non-white dependencies would, one by one, become independent. In effect, Commonwealth inter-dependency could no longer remain a white affair only, but had to become a multi-racial coalition – the opposite of apartheid. And in the face of opposition from African states, India, and Canada, South Africa withdrew from the Commonwealth in 1961.

South Africa's withdrawal spoke to a long existing tension within the Commonwealth, namely, its racialized division between self-governing subjects and dependent populations. As the Cold War began, some imperial reformers worried that this division might push independence leaders toward the Soviet Union. We've come across this anxiety in the last chapter; and Bronislaw Malinowski was a contemporary of Smuts. Just two years after the beginning of formal apartheid, Harry Hodson, a collaborator of Chatham House and a distinguished colonial administrator, articulated exactly the same fear:

> If communism succeeded in enlisting most of the discontented of the non-European races on its side, so that the frontier between democracy and its enemies was a racial

as well as an ideological and political frontier – then that danger would be greatly multiplied, and the chance of our eventually coming out on top would be so much the poorer. (Hodson 1950)

Remember the image of international politics that I gave you: crossing lines, one horizontal and marking the inter-dependency of civilized polities; another set of lines, vertical and representing the hierarchical dependencies that typified imperial administration. The Commonwealth's model of good imperial governance was based on exactly this racialized combination of equality and hierarchy: inter-dependence for white peoples and polities; dependence for non-white peoples and subjects.

But could the Commonwealth model survive decoloniz-ation? Hodson, for one, was unsure: "we are in the cocoon stage," he mooted, "and who can tell what moth or butterfly will hatch?" We will now see how this question drove Wight's inquiry into international relations and his exploration of whether anarchy and war could be avoided by the members of an "international society."

International Society

A practicing Catholic, Wight embraced Christian pacificism as a youth. Actually, his pacificism extended to opposing the repressive nature of British colonialism. A young Wight (1936, 19) even argued that part of British peacemaking required "surrender of the crown colonies and mandates to international administration by the league." But this anti-colonial position seems to have shifted a good deal when, due to his conscientious objection to fighting in World War II, Wight found himself working with Margery Perham at Oxford University.

Perham was an incredibly influential writer and teacher of colonial administration, and she appeared on the BBC regularly. Similar to Hodson, Manning, Smuts and so many others of her generation, Perham believed in good imperial governance. She shared a commitment to the paternalistic tutelage of natives so as to put them on the long and gradual path toward self-governance. Perham also shared a fear of the native's reactionary and contagious potential of disorder. She even believed that male colonial subjects visiting England sought out inter-racial sex as an act of "supreme racial compensation" (Bailkin 2012, 110).

Perham clearly influenced Wight. During the 1940s, Wight began to write weighty treatises on imperial administration and the various kinds of dependent relations that the Commonwealth shared along with its inter-dependent self-governing parts. Above all, his Christian pacificism attracted to itself a new target: the potential violence borne of anti-colonial self-determination. For instance, Wight and other imperial reformers warned that, in the absence of enlightened white tutelage, struggles for independence might well end up producing an "African Hitler" (Hall 2015, 137).

In 1958 Wight joined a historian called Herbert Butterfield in using Rockefeller Foundation funding to set up a British Committee on the Theory of International Politics. (A similar Rockefeller funded conference had taken place in the US a few years prior.) Unlike the debates at Chatham House, the British Committee did not seek to directly influence foreign policy but rather to academically theorize the behavior of the diplomatic community whom Wight called the "international society." The Committee met three times a year at Cambridge University, and for their first meeting Wight wrote a provocative and very famous essay, "Why Is There No International Theory?"

With this essay Wight's focus seemed to shift. In it, his concerns for the Commonwealth and imperial reform almost disappeared. At best, they fell into the background. The narrative and analysis were instead mostly taken up with various musings on the European body politic and its ability to avert war and violence. The majority of Wight's subsequent writings on "international theory" were written in the same register.

On face value, it's a curious turn. Well, I'm going to argue that Wight's commitment to good imperial governance in the form of the Commonwealth fundamentally shaped his specific intellectual contributions to IR, especially the concept of "international society," but in ways that are not immediately obvious. To convince you of this reconceptualization, I'm going to provide some methods for looking beneath and besides the surface of texts to gain a deeper and broader interpretation. But before that, I will need to sketch out the most obvious features of Wight's theorization of international politics.

In "Why Is There No International Theory?," Wight proposed that international politics was "less susceptible to a progressive interpretation" than domestic politics. Picking up on that old distinction I mentioned above concerning the European "family of nations" and its outsiders, Wight (1966b) noted that, historically, the European family had collectively enjoyed the "good life" and the progress that came with it. Outside of this family, however, international politics remained for him the "realm of recurrence and repetition."

In Wight's view of international politics, the specificity of the European family of nations as a civilized enclave of humanity took on great importance. He charted Europe's history beginning with the way in which Latin Christendom had existed from the eleventh to early sixteenth centuries as a "single juridical unit." Internally, this unit was comprised of a diverse array of polities inter-dependent upon each other; externally, it faced Islam and the Byzantine Empire (Wight 1946, 23). Modern-day international politics began, argued Wight, when this "Christian unity" came to an end. The French Revolution of 1789 introduced the non-religious principle of national self-determination, which fractured the old Christian unity.

Wight claimed that the replacement of religious unity by national self-determination made the pursuit of peace, justice, and order on an international scale that much harder to ensure. More fundamentally, he proposed that this historical transformation challenged the moral criteria by which the Christian diplomats and statesmen who comprised "international society" enacted foreign policy. Consequently, after the end of Latin Christendom, it would be idealistic to imagine that humanity could gather again in the same moral universe, whether through religion or ideology. And with the establishment of the principle of national self-determination, it was just as idealistic to imagine the rise of one empire to rule them all.

This being the case, Wight suggested that the best that international society could do in the modern era was to exercise restraints upon its members. Taking the middle ground between reckless self-interest and hopeless universalism, Wight imagined that a collective of diplomats and statesmen could help to maintain a balance of power between nations. The tools of diplomacy – treatises and international law – might not be able to stop war, but they could help to better regulate social, technical, and economic interdependence. In these ways and to this extent, Wight believed that the Christian-originated unity of the diplomatic world might still provide a residual influence in mitigating war and violence world-wide (Wight 1966a, 96).

It's an elegant argument. But if religious belief no longer provided the rationale and impetus for doing good in the world, or at least diminishing the bad, then what compelled diplomats and statesmen to undertake this moral endeavor?

Wight proposed that morality was still practiced in international society via a lingering commitment to natural law. Wight described the natural-law tradition in terms of a pre-Christian philosophy retrofitted during the Renaissance to secularize biblical commandments. According to this tradition, implanted in nature were ethical directives for the building of a just political order. The surviving commitment to such directives, even if not obviously religious, provided diplomats with an understanding that doing what was "expedient" for their own polity was not necessarily the same as doing what was "good" for humanity (Wight 1966a, 123). Expedient and short-term policies had to be "tempered" to some degree by ethical concerns for long-term arrangements.

Thus, Wight proposed that if international society was not a sovereign order with legal efficacy, it could nonetheless mitigate the worst excesses of anarchy with the force of moral convention. Given these commitments, he proposed that diplomats and statesmen were compelled to hold their offices of government as a trust. That is, those who governed should not act on their own short-term interest but for the long-term posterity of the governed. This kind of trusteeship, noted Wight, required "prudence" (Wight 1966a, 127–128). Prudential foreign policy making took shape as the "permissible accommodation between moral necessity and practical demands" (Wight 1966a, 129). Happily, this meant that moral issues could be pursued prudentially without the need for disorder and revolutionary upheaval.

For Wight, these were the principles of good governance that international society could and should abide by and promote. And do they not sound to you like the principles of good *imperial* governance that many of Wight's generation were supportive of? Let me now try to convince you that the resonance in Wight's writings between governance through international society and governance through the Commonwealth model was less of a coincidence and more a case of shared colonial logic.

There are a number of ways to interpret writings. The "intra-textual" strategy looks at the connections between logics, statements, and arguments within the text itself; the "inter-textual" strategy looks at these connections between different texts of the author as well as the wider conversation of books and letters that she is part of; and the "inter-locutory" strategy looks at the non-textual and non-intellectual logics, statements, and arguments that exist in the world of public debate that the author is working in.

So, let's think about the interlocutory – the world of public debate. In Wight's Britain, that debate is primarily framed by the challenge of letting empire finish in an orderly fashion such that its ex-members might still hold commitments to Britain. In these debates, the Commonwealth model looms large as that which assures the continuation of good imperial governance even after the end of empire.

Now think about the inter-textual. Wight's comments about diplomacy and trusteeship are made shortly after he publishes books that map out the practice of good imperial governance. Henceforth, this map is used to navigate the academic discourse of international politics via a historical analysis of international society. The special values held by European diplomats and statesmen – prudence, inter-dependency, trusteeship – are exactly those values that underwrite the Commonwealth model of good imperial governance.

Finally, think about the intra-textual. Here, we can focus specifically on the selection of examples that demonstrate the logic of the text's argument. Recall that the outside of international society, just like the European family of nations, is marked by different behavior and expectations of conduct. At various points in his texts, Wight illuminates the challenges facing international society by reference to South Africa and its pariah status after leaving the Commonwealth. For instance, Wight (1946, 105), makes mention of Afrikaner diplomats and statesmen who, by recusing themselves from shared Commonwealth values, "sought isolation and freedom from the shackles of international obligation."

It's plausible, then, to claim that Wight presented "international society" as the analogue to the Commonwealth of Nations. I'm now going to argue something even more audacious. It might well be this analogue that explains Wight's pronounced pessimism as to the future of international politics and the recurrence of war and violence. For Wight's writings on international politics, published between the 1950s and early 1970s, were overshadowed by the terminal decline of Britain as a global imperial power.

The sun set on the British Empire in two ways. Firstly, in July 1956, Britain failed to gain US backing for an attempt to reverse President Nasser of Egypt's nationalization of the Suez Canal, which Britain and France had previously owned. After Suez, Britain could no longer pretend that it could project its power globally, as it did during its imperial heyday. Secondly, and even more fundamentally, Britain lost its influence as a military and economic pivot for the "old" white-majority Commonwealth members. The ANZUS defense treaty of 1955 wedded Australia and New Zealand closer to the US and without including Britain. By the 1960s, the same realignment was clearly underway in economic terms, as Britain, suffering a balance of payments deficit, sought closer ties with the European Economic Community.

It's extremely telling that Wight makes explicit his concerns over anti-colonial self-determination in two publications that book-end this era of terminal imperial decline. The first text was published in 1946, just after he finished working with Margery Perham at Oxford. As a result of observing the first sessions of the United Nations as a journalist, Wight wrote a treatise on *Power Politics*. There, he argued that the principle of national self-determination, which had been introduced by the French Revolution and had done so much to shatter the religious unity of Europe, was now expanding in Asia and Africa through the decolonization movement against "European domination" (Wight 1946, 27). However, I want to focus on the second text – a journal article Wight published in 1972, the year of his death. In it, Wight (1972) made a last effort to salvage the Commonwealth model with a discussion on "international legitimacy."

At this late point in his life, Wight seems to have been especially interested in the dangerous populism associated with anti-colonial self-determination. Roughly speaking, populism pertains to the justification of sovereign authority as the general will of the "people." Wight proposed that anti-colonial populism was a response to two features of European imperialism. Firstly, colonies tended to be overseas from the imperial center. And secondly, most colonies were ruled via a small administrative minority that separated themselves from the racially distinct native "tribes." To pursue anti-colonial self-determination on behalf of the "people" was therefore to pursue territorial wholeness and majority rule.

Wight (1972, 17) pointed out that colonialism was apprehended by native elites, and in the words of Indian independence leader Krishna Menon, as a "permanent aggression" against the people. By this reckoning, no existing political arrangements could survive decolonization: everything had to be reset and begun again for the people to become truly self-governing. The problem, Wight argued, was that due to the populist focus on territorial integrity and majority rule, the pursuit of self-determination could easily justify new violence, war, and injustices. For instance, ruling native elites could claim their "tribe" as the "majority" people against other "minority" tribes. What's more, newly independent states could use the principle of territorial integrity to justify land grabs in adjacent polities, themselves becoming imperialist.

To be clear: Wight was not empirically wrong. These trajectories often did materialize after independence. Even Frantz Fanon warned of such deleterious consequences, and long before Wight did. The point of contention is rather to do with Wight's explanation of these post-colonial twists and turns. Above all, he shared the colonial logic of so many of his Cold War generation: without Western stewardship, anti-colonial self-determination would destabilize Western interests, which he associated with international society. For instance, Wight worried that the mass entrance of native elites into the UN, as colony after colony became independent, would lead to the organization promoting revolution instead of suppressing it. Communist principles, he asserted, held more in common with the 1960 UN Declaration on the Granting of Independence to Colonial Countries and Peoples than it did with the values that he attributed to international society. Wight saw independence and not colonialism as the problem.

Wight contrasted the principle of *populist* legitimacy with his commitment to government as *elite* trusteeship on behalf of the people. In this regard, he sought to counter anti-colonial populism with an older principle of legitimate rule more conducive to trusteeship – "prescription." Teasing out the political meaning of prescription, Wight turned to a famous eighteenth-century conservative thinker, Edmund Burke. An Irish politician who became an English member of parliament, Burke lambasted the French Revolution, defended the idea of orderly and piecemeal change, and considered empire as the most positive force for such change (Kohn and O'Neill 2006). "Through long usage," Burke asserted, "[prescription] mellows into legality governments that were violent in their commencement" (Wight 1972, 3). In short, the principle of prescription affirmed the maxim: *ex injuria jus oritur* – out of injustice, justice can arise.

Wight sought to legitimize imperial rule through the principle of prescription. The beginnings of empire in dispossession, enslavement, violence, and oppression might not determine its future arrangements. Out of colonial injustice, a commonwealth justice could arise – albeit a tutelary kind of justice, that is, one determined by a protector or guardian. The course of justice should not be determined by those colonized peoples who were wronged. Rather, it would be provided by the trustees of international society who followed the dictates of natural justice via the application of prudence.

Let's recap for a moment. At the start of this chapter I described the European "family of nations" as a crosscutting of two kinds of lines: one, horizontal and comprised of interdependent relations between polities; the other set of lines, vertical and comprised of each empire's governing structure. Outside of these crossing lines lay savagery and anarchy. I also noted that the Commonwealth was conceived as a kind of mini family of nations with a consonant crisscrossing logic of governance. The maintenance of inter-dependence for some and tutelage for others was the design that lay at the heart of Commonwealth governance in its effort to provide the "good life" for a multi-racial posterity. Beyond the imperial design lay dangerous principles that could lead to war and violence such as anti-colonial self-determination and the self-rule of non-white peoples.

Wight's "international society" was similarly crossed with inter-dependence and dependence. The society was not only comprised of a small set of diplomats and statesmen, who shared a moral commitment to government as a trust and who treated each other with some kind of parity; it was also a society that accepted the hierarchies of empire, and that sought to moderate the dangerous and disorderly pursuit of popular global justice with tutelary prudence. International society was a model to conserve good imperial governance in the end days of European empire, when that model had been lost even in the halls of the UN.

This was the source of Wight's conservative pessimism, which informed his "international society" approach. Even as the Commonwealth was being sidelined, Wight could not conceive of any other alternative to the Commonwealth model. Only this model might mitigate the slide into yet more war and violence made inevitable by the pursuit of populist anti-colonial self-determination. In taking this position, Wight could not imagine that the salvation of humanity from war and violence might come from a different kind of international society forged by the colonized themselves.

A Nuclear-Free and Independent Pacific

Martin Wight's characterization of international society certainly seems naive to twenty-first-century readers. In the context of globalization, how could you count the membership of this society in terms of a small coterie of statesmen and diplomats? Far more importantly, what about the existential threats we now face that make a mockery of traditional diplomacy and state power? Pandemics and the climate crisis come immediately to mind.

But fears of imminent global catastrophe are not at all new. The prospect of nuclear war shadowed the entire Cold War, and IR as a subfield was obsessed with the possibility of Armageddon. Even in his famous essay, "Why Is There No International Theory?," Wight wondered whether the creation of nuclear weaponry had fundamentally transformed international politics. He was by no means alone. The next year, Henry Kissinger (1960), as director of the Harvard Defence Studies Program, argued that nuclear weapons made any strategy of limited war extremely difficult. By the early 1980s, popular scientists such as Carl Sagan presented evidence that nuclear war would have devastating environmental consequences, most likely resulting in a prolonged "nuclear winter" (Turco et al. 1983).

However, much of the opposition to the nuclear arms race came from the peripheries of domestic and international politics. This is not surprising, considering that the first nuclear powers – the USA, UK, France, China, Soviet Union – all found locations for weapons testing either in the most isolated parts of their military empires or near displaced or unvalued populations in their own states (Jacobs 2013; see also Biswas 2001). For the US, that meant the Marshall Islands as well as in Nevada on the lands of Western Shoshone and South Paiute peoples and down-wind from Mormon communities; for Britain, Western Australia; for France, Algeria, and then French Polynesia; for the Soviet Union, the steppes on the edge of the Chinese border; for China, Lop Nur, close to the predominantly Muslim and minority ethnic Uyghur peoples (who have recently suffered ethnic cleansing by the Chinese Communist Party).

Calling attention to the dangerous influence of anti-colonial movements in the halls of global governance, Wight made derogative mention of what he called the "Bandung UN" (Hall 2014, 972). He was referencing perhaps the most important meeting of Asian and African states during the Cold War, which took place in 1955 at Bandung, a city in Indonesia. In his opening speech to the conference, Indonesian President Sukarno (1955) urged Asian and African peoples, the "majority" of humanity, to make a forceful moral argument for disarmament and peace. The same anti-nuclear stance was present in many of the regional groupings that subsequently accompanied decolonization. For instance, in a speech at the formation of the Organization of African Unity in 1963, Emperor Haile Selassie I of Ethiopia (1963, 289–290) pushed for an end to nuclear testing and a progressive disarmament.

These calls for denuclearization were also picked up by marginalized peoples living within the borders of great powers. For example, the Baltimore Afro-American newspaper reported that "amid all the rattling of nuclear weapons, if [Bandung] does no more than hold out a slim hope for [peace,] this greatest of all human desires, all mankind could rejoice and call it blessed" (Intondi 2019, 84). Meanwhile, Merze Tate, the first African-American woman to gain a PhD in government and international relations from Harvard University co-wrote an examination of the effect of nuclear testing on the peoples of the Marshall Islands (Tate and Hull 1964).

Teresia Teaiwa, a famous feminist scholar of Pacific Studies, draws our attention to the Bikini – the swimsuit launched by French designer Louis Reard in 1946. Bikini is also the name of an atoll in the Marshall Islands, designated in 1946 as the first US site for post-war nuclear weapons testing. At the time, military authorities described the atoll as comfortably remote and its small population as "primitive" and easily removable. Teaiwa's (1994) point is that when we think of Bikini, we tend to imagine a depoliticized and eroticized female body, which distracts us from the "colonial and highly political origins of its name." And just consider the history of what came to be known as the Marshall Islands: they had first been claimed by Spain in the late sixteenth century, partially transferred to the German Empire in the late nineteenth century, occupied by the Japanese Empire during World War I, and taken by the US in World War II.

Following Teaiwa's direction, we're going to examine how the struggle against nuclear testing in the Pacific was highly political in so far as it was also an anti-colonial movement in which Pacific women were key strategists and activists. In doing so, we'll arrive at a fundamental reimagination of the causes of war and prospects for peace to that proffered by Wight.

In 1970, around the time that Wight was writing his last publication, Fiji gained independence from the British Empire. Immediately, campaigning by students and church members sought to turn the new state's foreign policy toward an anti-nuclear position. In 1975, the Against Tests in Mururoa Committee (ATOM), and other regional groups, organized the first International Conference for a Nuclear-Free Pacific in Fiji's capital city, Suva. Eighty-six organizations from twenty-two Pacific nations and two European states participated.

Here's the thing. The conference did not wait for the tutelary governance provided by an "international society" of diplomats and statesmen. As well as promulgating seventeen resolutions, and sending messages to regional organizations including the Organization of African Unity, the conference drafted a "People's" Treaty for a Nuclear-Free Pacific Zone. The treaty sought a test-free zone stretching from Latin America, to Antarctica, to the Indian Ocean, including Micronesia and Australia. That, by the way, is an area significantly larger than the Earth's landmasses combined. Initially, the conference downplayed the importance of colonial legacies. The Campaign for Nuclear Disarmament New Zealand (CND-NZ) was a key organizer of the Fiji Conference and was part of a vibrant peace movement that had been galvanized in the 1960s both by New Zealand's entry into the Vietnam War and by British nuclear testing in Australia. Yet the movement was predominantly Pākehā led. (Pākehā is a Māori word that conventionally translates as "white settler.")

In terms of its anti-nuclear stance, CND-NZ enjoyed some support from the New Zealand state, which was a founding signatory of the 1968 non-proliferation treaty and a supporter of test-bans. In 1975, New Zealand joined Fiji and Papua New Guinea in writing to the UN Secretary General to push for a Nuclear Weapons Free Zone. In 1984, New Zealand became the second state after newly independent Vanuatu to refuse docking rights to US nuclear vessels. But New Zealand was also a settler-colony. That, as we shall see, significantly compromised its Pākehā-led peace movement.

Perhaps due to the strong influence of CND-NZ, discussions at the 1975 Fiji Nuclear-Free Conference began by focusing on the regional environmental consequences of weapons testing. Yet by the end of the proceedings, concern had pivoted to the colonial legacies and racist structures that enabled nuclear testing. After all, if Pacific peoples were not deemed disposable, and if nuclear powers did not have the use of islands and atolls taken through imperial ventures, then testing could never have taken place. The press release that accompanied the end of the conference reflected these evolving concerns:

> … racism, colonialism and imperialism lie at the core
> of the issue of the activities of the nuclear powers in
> the Pacific. The Pacific peoples and their environment

continue to be exploited because Pacific islanders are considered insignificant in numbers and inferior as peoples. (Naidu 1986, 7)

The conference met again in 1978 at Pohnpei, Micronesia, and in 1980, at Kailua, Hawai'i. By this point, the agenda was clearly led by indigenous peoples and their concerns for a Nuclear-Free *and* Independent Pacific (NFIP). A People's Charter was adopted, which bound the peace movement to decolonization. Calling out the environmental degradation begun with colonialism, but reaching cataclysmic levels with nuclear testing, the Charter committed the peoples of the Pacific to wresting control "over the destiny of our nations and our environment from foreign powers, including the Trans National Corporations." The 1983 NFIP conference, held in newly independent Vanuatu, further committed to anti-colonial struggle, including those taking place at the time in East Timor and West Papua against Indonesian colonization.

Recall that Wight feared the populism of anti-colonial self-determination for its tendency to incite more war and violence. And what was the NFIP but an avowedly peoples' movement! Well, I'm going to argue that Wight's fears were misplaced. The reason, I'll suggest, is in good part because it was driven by Pacific women. Just to be clear, I'm not making any essentialist claim about the peaceful nature of women. Instead, I want to introduce the notion of "intersectionality," first popularized in black feminist critique by Kimberlé Crenshaw (2015), a legal scholar. For our purposes, I'm going to focus on the work of another black feminist scholar, Patricia Hill Collins, who shifts intersectional analysis from legal discrimination to "oppression" more broadly conceived.

Collins (1990) criticizes "additive" models of oppression that, in her opinion, are rooted in the "either/or dichotomous thinking of Eurocentric, masculinist thought." Such thinking would accept that you could be oppressed either for your gender or your race, but not for both. As an alternative, Collins presents the idea of a "matrix of domination." Within this matrix there are a number of different "axes of oppression" that come together based on one's location in various societal structures. Collins is keen to point out that these axes of oppression are all quite specific: for example, race, class and gender articulate in very particular ways in the USA to oppress black women. Basically, we do not all suffer the same kind of oppression.

However, Collins is just as keen to argue that all axes of oppression necessarily interconnect. All axes are part of a wider matrix of domination. Hence, for Collins, intersectional analysis is necessary in order to carefully build meaningful solidarity with and across oppressed groups. Yet this is a process that requires consistent and careful self-reflection: we ourselves could be an oppressor along one axis while simultaneously an oppressed along another axis. Put another way, when we seek to resist oppression and build solidarity we must also resist the oppressor "within each of us."

Recall, for a moment, the image of crosscutting lines that help us to understand good imperial governance: a horizontal line representing inter-dependency for equals, and a set of vertical lines representing dependency for un-equals. Remember, also, Wight's preference for a tutelary style of global imperial governance: there are some who know what it takes to maintain order as well as pursue justice prudently; and there are others who need to be taught how to do so instead of independently pushing for a disorderly and ultimately bloody independence.

Now, contrast that image with the matrix of domination. Comprised of various axes of oppression, all of which intersect at multiple angles, the matrix does not separate equals from un-equals nor does it support self-governance for some and tutelage for others. Rather, to confront domination requires a general self-reflectivity from *everyone* caught up in its axes of oppression.

An intersectional analysis can help us to reimagine international politics as comprised of various axes of oppression within a matrix of domination. The NFIP is a case in point. We're going to see how those who were disproportionately driving the NFIP movement – Pacific women – were arguably far more self-reflective in their understanding of power than the members of Wight's international society – male, elite diplomats. And if prudence implies a care and concern for a future in shared trust, then perhaps Pacific women were far more prudent with their prescriptions of peace than those who believed in tutelage models of good imperial governance.

Let me give you one quick example of what kind of power relations an intersectional analysis might expose. Bill Ethel, an ex-military English man who had migrated to Australia, attended the Hawai'i Nuclear-Free Conference in 1980. Subsequently, he and his wife Lorraine raised monies with trade union and church support to buy a yacht, the *Pacific Peacemaker*. The yacht would raise publicity for the anti-nuclear peace movement by sailing into waters where nuclear testing or arms deployments were occurring.

In 1982, Mei Heremaia, a Pacific woman, joined the *Pacific Peacemaker* crew in their mission to break through the twelve-mile limit that the French had placed around their prime test site at Moruroa. Heremaia subsequently reported the misogynistic and racist environment that she faced on board. For instance, Ethel, the skipper, patronizingly asked her to "stay below with the kids" instead of taking part in political actions (Awatere and Heremaia 1982). For Heremaia, the clear message she received from her experience was that Pacific women were not supposed to take meaningful part in the struggle over the Pacific. This recollection demonstrates that a strong colonial attitude could be present even among those white men who put their life on the line to stop nuclear testing.

Collins points out that intersectional analysis is not an academic invention but rather something put into practice by social movements. So, we will now reconstruct the history of the NFIP with an intersectional analysis. For this purpose, I'm going to rely mainly on the archives that I collected during my years working in New Zealand. And I'm going to focus specifically on Māori and Pasifika women from that country. Māori, by the way, are the indigenous peoples of New Zealand, which in their language is called Aotearoa; today's Pasifika population mostly migrated to the country from the

1960s onwards, often from islands that the New Zealand state had some kind of historical imperial relationship with. Let's return to Fiji, 1975, and pick up the thread there. Amelia Rokotuivuna, an indigenous Fijian feminist, oversees logistics for the first nuclear-free conference. Her stewardship is not random but part of a broader resurgence of women's rights movements in the Pacific. One year before the meeting in Fiji, a Pacific Women's conference has convened in Port Moresby, Papua New Guinea. There, the definition of what counts as "women's issues" is expanded from care and home work to political and regional issues (Griffen 1976). The next such conference, held in October 1975, issues a communiqué in support of the People's Treaty drafted at the first Nuclear-Free Pacific Conference, just six months earlier.

Titewhai Harawira and Hana Te Hemara (also known as Hanna Jackson), both key activists in the Māori land movement, are present at the 1975 Nuclear-Free Conference in Fiji. Te Hemara also attends the women's conference there six months later. Recall that CND-NZ play a prominent role in the organizing of the event. After the conference, Te Hemera provides an intersectional reflection on Māori women's relationship to the largely Pākehā feminist contingent of New Zealand's peace movement (Griffen 1976).

Te Hemera argues that Māori women are "victims of both the racism and sexism of Pākehā society," and thereby "doubly discriminated against." Moreover, because Māori are disproportionately inserted into the low end of the white-settler capitalist economy, Māori women also have to fight for their family's economic survival. For Te Hemera, Māori women in the peace movement are positioned within specific axes of oppression incorporating colonialism, racism, patriarchy, and poverty. In contrast, the oppression suffered from the largely middle-class Pākehā women in the movement comes mostly from patriarchy.

Te Hemera's intersectional stance is also shared by Māori women who establish an indigenous-led nuclear-free and independent movement in New Zealand. In 1980, Hilda Halkyard-Harawira and Lis Marden attend the NFIP conference in Hawai'i. Returning to Auckland,

Halkyard-Harawira and Grace Robertson launch the Pacific People's Anti-Nuclear Action Committee (PPANAC) on August 6 – Hiroshima Day. (Heremaia actually represents PPANAC when she sails on the *Pacific Peacemaker.*)

PPANAC has two aims: to raise awareness of nuclear issues within the Māori community, and to "give an indigenous perspective" to the issue within New Zealand's mostly white anti-nuclear peace movement. Initially, PPANAC finds it difficult to convince other Māori activists that solidarity with the wider Pacific nuclear-free and independent movement is necessary and important for their own domestic struggle. This sentiment diminishes after PPANAC organizes an international meeting, Te Hui Oranga o Te Moana Nui a Kiwa (the meeting of Pacific survivors), at Tātai Hono Marae in Auckland.

But PPANAC finds it far harder to convince Pākehā activists of the same message (Halkyard-Harawira and Boanas 1992). Pākehā seem comfortable talking about French colonialism in Tahiti, but unable to connect the issues to the settler colonialism in which they are unavoidably and intimately entangled: the land struggle in New Zealand. The Māori activists of PPANAC understand that they have to resist oppression along multiple axes that include misogyny, eroticization (just think back to the Bikini), racism, poverty, and colonial dispossession. But Pākehā activists find it difficult to conceive that they might be the avatars of oppression as much as the purveyors of peace.

I mentioned above an aspect of Collins's intersectional argument, which advocates a self-reflective analysis of power, being that there might exist an "oppressor in each of us." Collins also argues that evidence of this sophisticated analysis of power can be found in the "alternative communities" of empowerment that black women have often created. This phenomenon is, perhaps, a global one. At least, there is clear evidence of such self-reflective analysis in the alternative communities that Māori activists create as part of the NFIP movement.

Te Hemera notes that, due to their experience of different axes of oppression, Māori women have to make more complex commitments of solidarity than their white feminist colleagues. Despite elements of patriarchy existing within Māori whānau (family) and iwi (tribe), Māori women suffer alongside their men when it comes to defending their "communalist" culture, which is under "increasing attack from Pākehā society." In any case, women have always been involved in Māori politics at the leadership level. Alternatively, the strict patriarchal politics imposed by the settler-colonial model of society led many Pākehā peace organizations to assign women merely to the role of "teamaker."

For these very tangible reasons, Te Hemera argues that Māori women are predisposed to pursue peace in more salient and consequential ways than Pākehā women. Again, this is not because of some innate capacity, but because "peace" for Māori women is intrinsically and necessarily an intersectional pursuit. Not only must nuclear testing be eradicated, but so too must settler colonialism, the capitalist economy, and patriarchy. Te Hemera suggests that Pākehā people need to undertake some serious self-reflection on what they take "peace" to be comprised of. Only then might they work in solidarity with Pacific women, a process that Te Hemera promotes through a traditional Māori whakataukī (proverb): "nāu te rākau, nāku te rākau, ka mate te hoariri" – "with your help and with our help the oppressor will be vanquished."

PPANAC activists are guided by similar understandings of solidarity and resistance to focus their movement on the various facets of militaristic imperialism. The "imperialist powers," they argue, are preparing for World War III, and they need land and sea to practice their testing and dispose of their waste – albeit "someone else's land and sea." Such powers have always been happy to foul, contaminate, and poison the "bodies, homes, islands, and waters" of Pacific peoples, whom they determined to be dispensable. The only way for islands to become "nuclear free" is thus to redress the "illegal" way in which indigenous lands have been stolen, whether by the abrogation of treaties signed by imperial powers or by the genocidal clearance enacted by white settlers.

To use Collins's language, PPNAC identify in the continuation of imperialism-via-militarism the matrix of domination through which all oppressions are interconnected. This is why PPANAC is adamant that nuclear testing cannot be sufficiently redressed as a one-dimensional issue, as many Pākehā activists presume. The struggle has to aim for "the kind of peace everyone can enjoy" – even the indigenous peoples of the Pacific. That means independence, or at least, self-governance over indigenous resources – and in Aotearoa New Zealand, as well.

PPANAC are skeptical that Pākehā allies can understand the depth of commitment necessary for peace to be meaningfully pursued on the world stage. Neither colonial dispossession nor the racism it breeds features in Pākehā axes of oppression – even among white feminists. "Whites," note PPANAC, "will always have the privilege of fighting racism when it suits them. We have no choice." Nonetheless, and echoing Te Hemera, PPANAC activists still hold to the intersectional principle that all struggles are interconnected: "So remember, we must fight hard to stop all forms of oppression."

Recall that Wight had hoped imperial rule would transform into an international society of tutelage, designed to moderate the aims and methods of postcolonial independence. Wight based his argument on the importance of "prescription": an arrangement that had begun with injustice could be prudently turned toward justice. Prudent diplomats and statesmen would hold the future in trust for humanity. Wight held out the slender hope that the Commonwealth might provide a model for such good imperial governance. And New Zealand was one of the original members of the Commonwealth. But under the guise of reform and enlightened leadership, the New Zealand state and white society pushed for peace in the Pacific without sufficiently connecting that push to redress the injustices of its own colonial situation.

Such a push came from those who were supposed to be most in need of tutelage: Māori and Pasifika peoples along with a few Pākehā and other allies. The momentous Māori Land March of 1975 was responsible for putting in place a Waitangi Tribunal charged with investigating breaches to the founding treaty between European settlers and Māori in 1840. The Treaty promised that Māori would retain governance over their lands, peoples, and cultures. Only one side took that promise seriously. After a decade of more struggle, the Treaty's mandate was extended retrospectively in 1984 to encompass the entire colonial history of breaches to the Treaty. Women activists such as Hana Te Hemara and Hilda Halkyard-Harawira wove the anti-nuclear peace movement into this land struggle.

These were the peoples and the forces that sought to repair the historical and contemporary injustices of settler-colonialism both in New Zealand and in the Pacific. They did so in order to bring, as famous New Zealand reggae band Herbs sang, the "Light of the Pacific" to a world under threat of nuclear annihilation. This was not the illumination provided by an elite international society tutoring wayward indigenous masses. It was, rather, the light of a prudential peoples' peace, a peace in trust, for generations past and generations to come, and one that could only be arrived at by the provision of global justice for the injustices of imperialism.

Conclusion

Of all the subfields of political science, I would argue that IR has experienced the greatest "decolonizing" impulse. Perhaps this is because of its direct history as a science of imperial administration. Perhaps it is also because the "good life" tends to forgo analysis of the "colonial life," and IR does not premise its analyses on the good life but on a world always verging on war and violence.

Critical scholars such as Mustapha K. Pasha were attempting to decolonize IR long before the phrase became popular. Recently, the Global Development section of the International Studies Association and the Colonial/Postcolonial/Decolonial working group of the British International Studies Association have become key sites wherein a collective decolonizing project has gained shape and focus. It might still be a marginal pursuit, but it is no longer a heresy to claim that you are trying to decolonize IR.

Still, that which makes IR open to decolonizing is also that which consistently seeks to obfuscate the need to decolonize the subfield. I am talking about the focus on existential survival, which necessarily comes with the study of war and violence. Raising the level of analysis to the level of human existence tends almost always to homogenize the diverse experiences of humans and smooth over the differing complicities of humans in the making of the problem itself. The climate crisis is a case in point.

Nowadays the crisis is used to demonstrate the inadequacy of focusing on state power in the era of the "Anthropocene" wherein human agency has altered weather patterns on a planetary scale. I have no desire to refute the scientific data on rising temperatures and waters. But I do question the assumption, so often accompanying this research, that this crisis is ethically unprecedented for humanity due to its existential nature. Indeed, some geographers have pointed out that the "Anthropocene" mis-identifies the crisis as a generically human one. It is, they propose, more accurately described as a masculine, patriarchal, racist, colonial one.

The colonization of the Americas, geographers propose, resulted in the "Orbis spike" of 1610. In this moment, ecosystems across continents first became intentionally interconnected on a planetary scale, from germs all the way up to humans; at the same time, the genocide of indigenous peoples actually produced a worldwide decrease in atmospheric carbon dioxide – that is, the gas that humans expel in the act of breathing (Davis and Todd 2017). Just imagine the scale of that ecological transformation and accompanying genocide. Was this not – does this not remain – a profoundly existential crisis of humanity? "We consider the future from what we believe is already a dystopia," argues Kyle Powys Whyte (2017), a Neshnabé scholar. The Pacific women activists who have fought for a nuclear-free *and* independent Pacific would, I am sure, understand that sense of the past and present.

Think back to Sylvia Wynter's argument concerning the overdetermination of the "human" with Man1 and Man2. A focus on existential crisis can easily and unintentionally hide the continuation of colonial logics by avoiding the question as to who has been included and excluded from the very category of humanity. But these logics start to emerge unavoidably when we ask: whose existential crisis is it, whose humanity is primarily at stake, and who suffers the most? These are questions that are germane to the subfield of IR but that require a decolonizing impulse to adequately address. Otherwise, we might assume that problems only require solving once they affect the elite classes at the so-called center of the world – those that colonialism always served well.

But it is not ridiculous to think that those at the margins, who have suffered these crises the longest, might provide the most edifying ideas and effective analyses concerning the redemption of humanity from war and destruction. This will be our principal consideration as we now finish our journey together.

–6–

Conclusion

We started with Aristotle, in ancient Greece. And we've traveled some distance, recontextualizing, reconceptualizing, and reimagining some of the core concepts, categories and issue areas of political science. At this point, it's worth collecting some thoughts on the commonalities that we've uncovered across the subfields we've examined. Actually, as I look back, I'm struck by how each subfield addressed the challenges of empire and colonialism by dividing humanity into oppositional categories with fixed properties. There is a colonial logic that repeats itself, albeit in different forms, across the whole discipline.

Consider, firstly, the chapter on political theory. There, we witnessed how philosophers used a distinction between properly human and not-properly human to make sense of what rights can be reasonably accorded to humanity in all its diversity. Secondly, political behavior. There, the distinction made by the science of race heredity enabled scholars to sort a diverse citizenry into those who properly presented normal behaviors fitting for democracy and those that did not. Similarly, comparative politics. The distinction between modern and traditional societies allowed comparativists to adjudicate which development trajectories of newly independent polities were well-adjusted and which were maladjusted. Fourthly, international relations. The racialized distinction between civilized politics and uncivilized peoples provided colonial administrators and their academic colleagues the justification for promoting good imperial governance as an answer to the endemic prospect of war and violence.

These colonial logics create binaries: idealized qualities or conditions that are defined in opposition to each other. The problem with these binaries is that, when it comes to imperial administration and colonial rule, they are forcibly attached to real people, collectivities, and places. The black person becomes intrinsically "irrational," the North African born with a "maldeveloped" psyche, the political systems of post-colonial states are categorized as hopelessly "traditional," while European diplomats are elevated as quintessentially "prudent."

True, every now and then in these writings the black person might show reason, the North African emotional maturity, the Third World government a scientific outlook, and Pacific women prudence. But this evidence is always met with suspicion and contingency: did the black person show his own reason or was he merely parroting a white man? Can all North Africans reach emotional maturity or was it just that individual? For how long will Third World governments demonstrate a scientific outlook? Someone must have taught Pacific women to be prudent – they couldn't have learned that by themselves. The point is that, once binaries have been attached to real people, collectives, and places, they become stubbornly immovable (see Santos 2013).

I started this book by gesturing to the "uncanny" as a combination of the familiar and unfamiliar, and the intimacy of this combination. Rehearsing Aristotle's life story I suggested that imperial expansion and the colonial project intimately shaped political concepts that we imagine are nothing to do with empire and colonialism – for instance, the "polis" itself. I hope you might understand now, at the end of our journey, how important it is for us to challenge these conventional binaries – not just for morality's sake, but for the sake of better analysis too.

Because the last chapter finished with the Pacific Nuclear-Free and Independent Movement, let me expand on this challenge by reference to the idea of "taboo." A "taboo" is usually understood to be a prohibition on an action, and its force is usually understood to arise from religious or spiritual sanction. Taboos often take on a sense of perversity, such as incest, eating human flesh, etc. The "nuclear taboo" pertains to the idea that, after the horror of Hiroshima and Nagasaki, no military power would ever use its nuclear arsenal in war due to the extreme stigma surrounding such a fundamentally inhuman and ungodly act.

The word taboo comes into the English language through James Cook, the infamous Pacific explorer and naval captain. Cook took it from a specific cluster of Pacific languages all of which have a word consonant to "tapu." In the Māori language (te reo), tapu is paired with "noa" (see in general Satterfield et al. 2005; Keelan and Woods 2006). Conventionally, this pairing is translated as sacred (tapu)/profane (noa). However, perhaps a more adequate translation would be charged (tapu)/neutral (noa).

Tapu and noa are paired in order to regulate the flow and intensity of life. There are moments, situations, actions, and places that are energetically charged, and where life is most immediately and intensely lived. But if we were to live life consistently "on" in this fashion we would exhaust ourselves completely and unbalance all our relations with humans and other entities. In the long spaces between these moments, situations, actions, and places we need to live neutrally. For example, when you enter a grave site, you are entering an energetically charged place. On leaving you need to wash so that you can neutralize yourself again.

Therefore, tapu should not be understood as a perverse, mystical action that is categorically distinct to normal actions. Rather, tapu is all about moving in and out of situations where our relationships are especially charged and consequential. It is a regulatory principle that crucial moments are given their due attention but do not take all the energy out of life. There is no such thing as a perverse "taboo" in distinction to a "normal" action of state of being.

Rather, there is a regulation of energy and power that shifts and morphs across people and places. Sometimes a person is tapu, and then the rest of the time she is noa. There's something uncanny about taboo. On the one hand, we all think we know instinctively what that word refers to, and we use that meaning to explain the use or prohibition of perhaps the most destructive energy that science has revealed to humanity. On the other hand, the very word is imbibed with a sense of exoticism and mysticsm. To put it another way, political scientists have addressed the nuclear issue with a concept that they themselves have made irrational and mystical; indigenous knowledge, meanwhile, demonstrates a rational and pragmatic engagement! That is uncanny.

Maybe you're getting a sense now of the tremendous effort that is required to contort peoples and places and contain them within binary opposites. Colonial logic must turn concepts such as "tapu" into "taboo." What I mean is that colonial logic refuses any consideration of peoples and places as flowing, shifting, and changing entities with relationships that increase and decrease in intensity. The dictates of imperial administration and colonial rule have always required the consistent fixing of a multi-faceted, moving, and relational reality. Fixing reality in this extreme way must require – or at least, must lead to – violence. Conceptualizing, diagnosing, and prognosing the political world by these same logics is part of this violence (see Castro-Gomez and Martin 2002).

There is an ethical and analytical cost to studying politics through colonial logics. Allow me to write a train of thoughts about this kind of logic-inducing-violence. I'm thinking of the ways in which "native" peoples and domestic "second-class" citizens are consistently ascribed an inability to rationalize – to think reasonably and competently for modern times. Across the subfields of political science, this ascription is inherited, sometimes implied, and often assumed. Irrationality breeds disorder and anarchy. Disorder and anarchy must be controlled or mitigated. Control and mitigation require violence. At best there can be long-term tutelage. That, though, requires order over justice.

And those native elites? They think that just because they've read the same books as us, studied or worked in the same institutions as us, that they are worthy of equal treatment. They are perhaps the most deluded. Regrettably, if tutelage fails, if these elites fail their own people, there is always apartheid. Not necessarily the "big-A" apartheid, as in South Africa but more mundane and informal separations and segregations of peoples, domestically and/or globally. Build a wall around a state. Build a wall around a neighborhood. Build a wall around your heart. Don't be naive. You're romanticizing the "Other." I'm sorry. We tried our best. But they just couldn't get it. For our best interests *and for theirs* we must govern and be governed differently. The continuum between brutal discipline and orchestrated neglect is broad enough to assuage every conscience.

I began this book by introducing Aristotle as an uncanny thinker of relations, of peripheries, of borders. Instead of a theorist of the fixed center, of the citizen in the polis, I noted that Aristotle, himself a marginal man in Athens, criticized imperial war. He worried that empires tended to produce despots that citizens would ultimately have to serve slavishly. I suggested that Aristotle's discussion of politics was an attempt to show Athenian citizens their own image refracted: here's what you believe and practice; here's the logic behind it; here's what might be the consequences; are you happy with that? I used Aristotle's uncanniness – his familiarity and unfamiliarity – to open up the prospect that even the "father" of political science was a critical thinker of imperial administration and colonial rule, the after-lives of which still structure our political world.

But I also demonstrated that Aristotle was profoundly conservative. There are more conservatisms than just the big-C ideology. And conservatism per se is not necessarily a bad thing; we all wish to conserve that which we think is good. The question is whether what we think is good requires the suppression of the good life for others. Kant was right: we should treat everyone as the ends rather than the means of action. It's just that Kant circumscribed this imperative only to the properly human – the white, rational, man.

Well, Aristotle wished to conserve the practice of citizenship; but this practice depended upon hierarchies of dependency wherein the labor of slaves and women allowed free time for the man to exercise his deliberative reason, in the absence of immigrants, in the agora – the public space of citizens and the debating arena of politics. And remember, many of Aristotle's political writings were responding to an anti-slavery movement that had been defeated but the message of which lingered on: if slavery was against natural law then the privileged status of citizenship enjoyed by some but not others was untenable.

I guess I'm saying that in order to decolonize the study of politics we can take Aristotle's cue; but as we proceed on our new journey, we might want to leave behind the hierarchies that the father of political science ultimately sought to preserve. I'm going to finish this book by engaging with the work of a cultural theorist who I think does just this, and whose work might be valuable to those of us who study politics.

For this purpose, I'm going to use a teaching technique that I learnt from Manjeet Ramgotra, a political theorist at SOAS. In her classes, Ramgotra convenes unlikely conversations between various thinkers. By these means, her students can test the bounds of conventional political science. For instance, Ramgotra assigns a reading from Plato and a reading from black feminist theorist bell hooks, and she tells the students to imagine the conversation between them.

Here's a final reimagining, then. We're going to put Aristotle in conversation with Gloria Evangelina Anzaldúa (1942–2004), a Chicanx queer theorist. Chicanx (a gender-neutral pronoun derived from Chicano/Chicana) describes those peoples living in the US who are of Mexican descent. Queer theory seeks to unsettle the binaries that are ascribed to peoples' personal and political identities, and to raise the possibility that there are multiple, perhaps endless, articulations of masculinity, femininity, and other expressions of being together.

Anzaldúa uses queer theory and her Chicanx history and heritage to confront the phenomenon that in politics represents perhaps the most consequential binary of all – the border. Anzaldúa tells the history of a specific border – that which divides the US and Mexico. She narrates this history not from the centralized perspective of the state but rather from the "borderlands." Her story begins with the ancient ancestors of the Chicanx peoples, who occupied or regularly migrated through the south-west of the US, an area originally known as Aztlán. In 1000 BCE these ancestors undertook one of a number of large migrations further to the south. In the sixteenth century the Spanish conquistadors conquered the ancestors' lands of settlement in what was named New Spain and is present-day Mexico. Before long, the indigenous population collapsed as violent land dispossession exacerbated the negative impact of new germs, diseases, and diets imported from Europe (Estes 2020). Mestizos, usually the progeny of Spanish fathers and indigenous mothers, had both Spanish immunity and indigenous heritage. They increasingly populated these colonized lands.

Some of those mestizos migrated (back) north to Aztlán lands alongside Spanish adventurers in search of gold. They became the people now called Chicanx. Part of these lands were called Texas, which then became part of the state of Mexico after its independence from Spain in 1821. White settlers from the US migrated illegally into Texas and challenged Mexico's sovereignty. In 1846 the US gained Texas from Mexico through war. Much of the land lived on by Mexicans was subsequently stolen by white settlers. A race war in 1915 led to further forced dispossession. Many Chicanx were reduced to sharecroppers – people who farm on another person's land.

Anzaldúa's (1987, 11) point is that the indigeneity of Chicanx is neither fixed nor essential but constituted through mixing and movement. "We have a tradition," she notes, "of long walks." The colonial response to this tradition of migration has been the dispossession of lands by settler-colonial forces. Home for Chicanx is now a "thin edge of barbwire" (Anzaldúa 1987, 13).

Conventionally, the border marks the limit of governmental authority, setting citizens off from non-citizens and drawing a line separating legal from non-legal residents. The border is the frontier of the good life. Aristotle shares something with Anzaldúa's story of Chicanx people. His experience as a non-citizen in Athens, even as an asylum seeker in present-day Turkey, enables him to proffer a critique of imperialism. Nonetheless, his critique is designed to preserve citizenship in the settler-colonial city. Anzaldúa is not interested in holding the center together, even from the margins. She wants to get rid of the very project of building and defending centers, a project that seems to have marginalization as its quintessential logic.

And so Anzaldúa conceives of the border less as a limit and more as a place that cultivates a particular kind of living. At the border "the lifeblood of two worlds" merges to form a "border culture." This culture is the product of those who are not supposed to be able to create anything of value: the supposedly irrational, abnormal, non-citizen, maladjusted, and uncivilized that we've seen created in the formative colonial logics of political science. Anzaldúa describes them as the "perverse, the queer, the troublesome, the mongrel, the mulato, the half-breed," etc. And the culture they create, she notes, is far from fixed but rather in a "constant state of transition."

For Anzaldúa, then, the border is both a place, a condition of being, and a psychic space. It is also a place/ space/psyche that is brought into being by oppression and violence, especially when it comes to indigenous women. This is a really important factor for Anzaldúa. There is no culture, colonial, pre-colonial or otherwise, that can claim innocence when it comes to oppression and violence. She reflects on her own childhood. She talks of the way in which culture is made by those in power – men. Women are only supposed to transmit culture, not create it. Aristotle agrees: the sperm forms shape from passive female matter. All this is consonant with the Catholic Church's insistence of the subordination of women to men. Organized religion codes woman as "carnal, animal, and closer to the undivine." Above all, the woman must be protected from the "Shadow-Beast" in herself. Man is coded as closer to the divine and the protector of woman. Deviance is a crime against God and man.

With these cultural strictures, there exist four options for women: remain a virgin until patriarchal marriage thereby becoming a good mother, take to the streets as a prostitute and be damned, escape to the Church to become a nun, or use education to forge a career and become autonomous. This last choice might seem most attractive, but it is a choice presented only to a tiny minority. Anzaldúa then provides three responses to these unattractive choices. Firstly, Chicana women can conform to the values of culture, even if they are oppressive, in order to avoid rejection. But this strategy pushes the oppressive nature of culture into the "shadows," waiting to return. Or secondly, Chicana women might stare directly at the Shadow-Beast, at the sexual lust and the desire for power and destruction that underpins the male hetero-sexual order. But ... is the Shadow-Beast actually what men say it is?

Anzaldúa describes how she herself has followed a third response. As a child she is rebellious. She hates constraints, even ones that are self-imposed. She talks of – and embraces the fact that she has – the Shadow-Beast in her. Choosing to be queer, a so-called "deviant," Anzaldúa realizes that the Beast is not what it is said to be. The duality that limits human nature to either male or female, divine or beast, is fundamentally challenged by "queer people." Anzaldúa (1987, 19) talks of herself as "two in one body, both male and female ... the coming together of opposite qualities within." For the "lesbian of color," the ultimate rebellion that she can make against her "native culture" is through her sexual behavior.

In actual fact, Anzaldúa considers this rebellion to be a reclamation of that culture – of its non-dualistic, mixed and migratory histories. Of course, counter-intuition requires counter-stories. Anzaldúa (1987, 21) argues that her Chicanx identity "is grounded in the Indian woman's history of resistance." She narrates a complex history of Coatlalopeub, a name given to the creator goddess of Mesoamerican fertility rites, and the mother of celestial deities. As a creator, she had both dark and light aspects that worked in relation to each other; and her creative power was also, necessarily, sexual and coiled. Interestingly, Coatlalopeub can be glossed as "the one who has dominion over serpents."

Anzaldúa recalls how the goddess was displaced by a "male-dominated Azteca–Mexica" culture. With this displacement the goddess became less of a being, her fullness attenuated – cut in half. Furthermore, the Catholic Church forbade all indigenous spiritual agents on account of them being associated with the devil. Except that the Church decided to disarm Coatlalopeub by associating her with La Virgen de Guadalupe, the form that the Virgin Mary took in Mexico, when it appeared to peasants in the sixteenth century. In these ways, the creator goddess was split from her dark and sexual energies and de-indigenized to become the "good mother." Still, Anzaldúa notes that La Virgen de Guadalupe retains some of Coatlalopeub's subversive aspects. To poor people, Guadalupe represents the pain of conquest and oppression, but also the hope and faith that comes with survival. Guadalupe also speaks to multiple races, religions, languages, and she mediates between Spanish, Indian, and African cultures.

Through the intercession of Guadalupe, Anzaldúa realizes that the Shadow Beast is what remains of Coatlalopeub after she has been diminished and demonized by both Aztec patriarchy and the Catholic Church. Embracing the fullness of the Beast, Anzaldúa seeks to renew the powers of Coatlalopeub, powers that do not reproduce dualisms of male and female, virtue and sexuality, reason and feeling, light and dark, citizen and alien, human and monster. This is why, choosing to be a "lesbian of color," Anzaldúa consistently proclaims throughout her book: "not me sold out my people but they me."

Aristotle was a critic of imperialism in so far as he feared the diminution of the good life that it would bring even upon those who practiced it. Nevertheless, this good life, for Aristotle, was predicated upon the hierarchies of the patriarchal household. These are the hierarchies that Anzaldúa wishes to leave behind as much as imperialism.

Reviving her Chicanx culture, Anzaldúa promotes a new mestiza consciousness – "a consciousness of the borderlands." Cultivated through the experience of oppression and violence, this consciousness does not seek out revenge but rather wishes to uproot binary thinking in order to bring an end to rape, violence and war. It is born of a feminist struggle that requires new masculinities.

Mestiza consciousness seeks to rupture oppressive traditions, re-narrate histories, re-interpret symbols. It wants to strengthen tolerance and ambiguity. It blends all blood so as to help bring into being a "broader communal ground" for all those who have experienced violent oppression. It even hopes that whites will stop trying to "help us" and realize that they need to "follow our lead" (Anzaldúa 1987, 85–87). Mestiza consciousness unravels the racial hierarchies of knowledge production. It reimagines the pursuit of what we call politics.

We can recontextualize and reconceptualize the intellectual roots and routes of political science. But without doing the work of reimagining, it's all too easy to re-center the center, even with the best of intentions. Most of the time, problems only become "real" problems when they hit the center, even if they have dwelt on and grown in and circulated around the borderlands for generations. Sensational news items – shoot outs, dirty deals, riots, wars etc. – usually represent the visible tip of political phenomena that grow behind doors, in back yards, down dirt tracks. I'm talking, for example, about the murder of intimate partners, the slow death suffered by poor people living in toxic environments, and experimentation in techniques of violence upon those who have no course to legal redress.

So, as you finish this book and wonder what to do next, here's a suggestion. Pick any issue discussed in the book – but it must be an issue that feels most intimate to you for whatever reason. Gather with others who feel the same way. Consider the colonial logics that underpin the political analysis of that issue. Think, then, about how a borderland consciousness might critique that analysis. Imagine what other divisions and separations such a critique would bring to the fore, and who or what might be the agents of repair. Spend some time and effort searching for these agents, past and/or present. (They might even have a presence within you and/or among your convened group.) Think about what you could offer them or their contemporary descendants/equivalents while they teach you. Take the bumps and scrapes that you might receive along the way in good faith. Imagine what practical and ethical structures would need to be put in place to make this relationship sustainable, equitable, honest, and care-full, during and after your time in the academy. And then pursue that solidarity, however you can.

References

Aberle, D. F., A. K. Cohen, A. K. Davis, M. J. Levy, and F. X. Sutton. 1950. "The Functional Prerequisites of a Society." *Ethics* 60 (2): 100–111.

Adams, Herbert B. 1882. *The Germanic Origin of New England Towns*. Baltimore: Johns Hopkins University.

Alford, John R., Carolyn L. Funk, and John R. Hibbing. 2005. "Are Political Orientations Genetically Transmitted?" *American Political Science Review* 99 (2): 153–167.

Almond, Gabriel A. 1956. "Comparative Political Systems." *Journal of Politics* 18 (3): 391–409.

Ambrosius, Lloyd E. 2007. "Woodrow Wilson and the Birth of a Nation: American Democracy and International Relations." *Diplomacy and Statecraft* 18 (4): 689–718.

Anagnostopoulos, Georgios. 2009. "Aristotle's Life." In *A Companion to Aristotle*, ed. Georgios Anagnostopoulos, 1–13. Oxford: Blackwell.

Anghie, Antony. 2005. *Imperialism, Sovereignty, and the Making of International Law*. Cambridge: Cambridge University Press.

Anzaldúa, Gloria. 1987. *Borderlands / La Frontera: The New Mestiza*. San Francisco: aunt lute books.

Aristotle. 2014. *Nicomachean Ethics*, ed. C. D. C. Reeve. Indianapolis: Hackett Publishing Company.

———. 2017. *Politics: A New Translation*, ed. C. D. C. Reeve. Indianapolis: Hackett Publishing Company.

Arrighi, Giovanni. 2009. "The Winding Paths of Capital:

Interview by David Harvey." *New Left Review* 56: 61–94.

Arrighi, Giovanni, and John S. Saul. 1968. "Socialism and Economic Development in Tropical Africa." *Journal of Modern African Studies* 6 (2): 141–169.

Awatere, Donna, and Mei Heremaia. 1982. "Peacemaker Politics." *Broadsheet*, December: 6–7.

Ayoob, Mohammed. 2001. "Humanitarian Intervention and International Society." *Global Governance* 7 (3): 225–230.

Bagehot, Walter. 1873a. *Physics and Politics*. New York: D. Appleton and Company.

———. 1873b. *The English Constitution*. Vol. 2. Boston: Little, Brown, & Co.

Bailkin, Jordanna. 2012. *The Afterlife of Empire*. Berkeley: University of California Press.

Bell, Duncan. 2007. *The Idea of Greater Britain: Empire and the Future of World Order, 1860-1900*. Princeton: Princeton University Press.

Bennett, Jane. 2010. *Vibrant Matter: A Political Ecology of Things*. Durham, N.C.: Duke University Press.

Bernasconi, Robert. 2001. "Who Invented the Concept of Race? Kant's Role in the Enlightenment Construction of Race." In *Race*, ed. R. Bernasconi, 11–36. Oxford: Blackwell.

Bhambra, Gurminder K. 2007. *Rethinking Modernity: Postcolonialism and the Sociological Imagination*. Basingstoke: Palgrave.

Bhambra, Gurminder, K., Dalia Gebrial, and Kerem Nişancıoğlu, eds. 2018. *Decolonising the University: Understanding and Transforming the Universities' Colonial Foundations*. London: Pluto Press.

Bhandar, Brenna. 2018. *Colonial Lives of Property: Law, Land, and Racial Regimes of Ownership*. Durham: Duke University Press.

Bilgin, Pinar, and Adam David Morton. 2002. "Historicising Representations of 'Failed States': Beyond the Cold-War Annexation of the Social Sciences?" *Third World Quarterly* 23 (1): 55–80.

Bisaha, Nancy. 2001. "Petrarch's Vision of the Muslim and Byzantine East." *Speculum* 76 (2): 284–314.

Biswas, Shampa. 2001. "'Nuclear Apartheid' as Political Position: Race as a Postcolonial Resource?" *Alternatives: Global, Local, Political* 26 (4): 485–522.

Blaney, David, and Naeem Inayatullah. 2002. "Neo-Modernization? IR and the Inner Life of Modernization Theory." *European Journal of International Relations* 8 (1): 103–137.

———. 2010. *Savage Economics: Wealth, Poverty, and the Temporal Walls of Capitalism*. London: Routledge.

Blatt, Jessica. 2018. *Race and the Making of American Political Science*. Philadelphia: University of Pennsylvania Press.

Booth, W. 1890. *In Darkest England and the Way Out* . London: Funk & Wagnal.

Bowden, Brett. 2005. "The Colonial Origins of International Law: European Expansion and the Classical Standard of Civilization." *Journal of the History of International Law* 7: 1–23.

Brooks, Jerome. 1994. "Chinua Achebe, The Art of Fiction," *The Paris Review* 133, https://www.theparisreview.org/interviews/1720/the-art-of-fiction-no-139-chinua-achebe.

Brown, Robert, and Cheryl Johnson. 1996. "Thinking Poetry: An Interview with Derek Walcott." In *Conversations with Derek Walcott*, ed. W. Baer, 175–188. Jackson: University Press of Mississippi.

Burden-Stelly, Charisse. 2017. "Constructing Deportable Subjectivity: Antiforeignness, Antiradicalism, and Antiblackness during the McCarthyist Structure of Feeling." *Souls* 19 (3): 342–358.

Burns, Tony. 2003. "The Tragedy of Slavery: Aristotle's Rhetoric and the History of the Concept of Natural Law." *History of Politcial Thought* 24 (1): 16–36.

Cambiano, Giuseppe. 1987. "Aristotle and the Anonymous Opponents of Slavery." In *Classical Slavery*, ed. Moses I. Finley, 28–52. London: Cass.

Camic, Charles. 1986. "The Matter of Habit." *American Journal of Sociology* 91 (5): 1039–1087.

Cartledge, Paul. 1993. *The Greeks: A Portrait of Self and Other*. Oxford: Oxford University Press.

Campbell, Horace. 1991. "The Impact of Walter Rodney and Progressive Scholars on the Dar es Salaam School." *Social and Economic Studies* 40 (2): 99–135.

Castro-Gomez, Santiago and Martin, Desiree A. 2002. The Social Sciences, Epistemic Violence, and the Problem of the "Invention of the Other." Nepantla: Views from the South 3 (2): 269–285.

Chantiluke, Roseanne, Brian Kwoba, and Athinangamso Nkopo, eds. 2018. *Rhodes Must Fall: The Struggle to Decolonise the Racist Heart of Empire*. London: Zed Books

Charney, Evan, and William English. 2013. "Genopolitics and the Science of Genetics." *American Political Science Review* 107 (2): 382–395.

Claeys, Gregory. 2000. "The 'Survival of the Fittest' and the Origins of Social Darwinism." *Journal of the History of Ideas* 61 (2): 223–240.

Coleman, James S. 1986. "The Idea of the Developmental University." *Minerva* 24 (4): 476–494.

Collins, Patricia Hill. 1990. *Black Feminist Thought: Knowledge, Consciousness, and the Politics of Empowerment*. Boston: Unwin Hyman.

Connolly, William E. 2017. *Facing the Planetary: Entangled Humanism and the Politics of Swarming*. Durham: Duke University Press.

Crenshaw, Kimberle. 2015. "Demarginalizing the Intersection of Race and Sex: A Black Feminist Critique of Antidiscrimination Doctrine, Feminist Theory and Antiracist Politics." *University of Chicago Legal Forum* 1989 (1).

Cusicanqui, Silvia Rivera. 2015. *Sociología de la Imagen: Miradas Ch'ixi Desde la Historia Andina*. Buenos Aires: Tinta Limón.

Darwin, Charles. 1871. *The Descent of Man*. Vol. 1. New York: D. Appleton and Company.

Davis, Carole Boyce, and Fido, Elaine Savory. 1990. *Out of the KUMBLA: Caribbean Women and Literature*. Trenton N.J.: Africa World Press.

Davis, Heather, and Zoe Todd. 2017. "On the Importance of a Date, Or, Decolonizing the Anthropocene." *ACME: An International Journal for Critical Geographies* 16 (4): 761–780.

De Juan, Alexander, and Jan Henryk Pierskalla. 2017. "The Comparative Politics of Colonialism and Its Legacies: An Introduction." *Politics and Society* 45 (2): 159–72.

Dietz, Mary G. 2012. "Between Polis and Empire: Aristotle's Politics." *The American Political Science Review* 106 (2): 275–293.

"Draft Recommendations of the Conference on the Role of the University College, Dar es Salaam, in a Socialist Tanzania." 1967. *Minerva* 5 (4): 558–570.

Duster, Troy. 1990. *Backdoor to Eugenics*. New York, N.Y.: Routledge.

Easton, David. 1949. "Walter Bagehot and Liberal Realism." *The American Political Science Review* 43 (1): 17–37.

Engerman, David C. 2010. "Social Science in the Cold War." *Isis* 101 (2): 393–400.

Escobar, Arturo. 2007. "Worlds and Knowledges Otherwise." *Cultural Studies* 21 (2–3): 179–210.

Estes, Nick. 2020. "The Empire of All Maladies." *The Baffler*, July 2020. https://thebaffler.com/salvos/the-empire-of-all-maladies-estes.

Euben, Roxanne L. 2004. "Travelling Theorists and Translating Practices." In *What Is Political Theory?*, 145–173. London: Sage Publications.

Eze, Emmanuel Chukwudi. 1995. "The Color of Reason: The Idea of 'Race' in Kant's Anthropology." *The Bucknell Review* 38 (2): 200–241.

Fanon, Frantz. 1967. "Medicine and Colonialism." In *A Dying Colonialism*, 121–146. New York: Grove Press.

———. 1970. "The 'North African Syndrome.'" In *Toward the African Revolution*, 13–26. London: Penguin.

———. 1986. *Black Skin, White Masks*. London: Pluto Press.

———. 2018a. "Letter to the Resident Minister." In *Alienation and Freedom*, eds. Jean Khalfa and Robert J. C. Young, 433–436. London: Bloomsbury Academic Press.

———. 2018b. "Social Therapy in a Ward of Muslim Men:

Methodological Difficulties." In *Alienation and Freedom*, eds. Jean Khalfa and Robert J. C. Young, 353–372. London: Bloomsbury Academic Press.

———. 2018c. "The Meeting Between Society and Psychiatry." In *Alienation and Freedom*, eds. Jean Khalfa and Robert J. C. Young, 511–530. London: Bloomsbury Academic Press.

Ferguson, Adam. 1995. *An Essay on the History of Civil Society*. Cambridge: Cambridge University Press.

Fowler, James H., and Christopher T. Dawes. 2013. "In Defense of Genopolitics." *The American Political Science Review* 107 (2): 362–374.

Frank, Jill. 2004. "Citizens, Slaves, and Foreigners: Aristotle on Human Nature." *American Political Science Review* 98 (1): 91–104.

Galton, Francis. 1865. "Hereditary Talent and Character." *Macmillan's Magazine* 12: 157–166, 318–327.

Gelder, Ken, and Jane M. Jacobs. 1995. "Uncanny Australia." *Ecumene* 2 (2): 171–183.

Gibson, Nigel C, and Roberto Beneduce. 2017. *Frantz Fanon, Psychiatry and Politics*. London: Rowman & Littlefield International.

Gilman, Nils. 2007. *Mandarins of the Future: Modernization Theory in Cold War America*. Baltimore: Johns Hopkins University Press.

Gordon, Jane Anna. 2014. *Creolizing Political Theory: Reading Rousseau through Fanon*.

Gordon, Lewis R. 2005. "From the President of the Caribbean Philosophical Association." *Caribbean Studies* 33 (2): xv–xxii.

Griffen, Vanessa, ed. 1976. *Women Speak Out!: A Report of the Pacific Women's Conference, October 27–November 2*. Suva: Pacific Women's Conference.

Grovogui, Siba N'Zatioula. 1996. *Sovereigns, Quasi Sovereigns, and Africans: Race and Self-Determination in International Law*. Minneapolis: University of Minnesota Press.

Gunnell, J. 2013. "Social Science and Ideology: The Case of Behaviouralism in American Political Science." In *The*

Oxford Handbook of Political Ideologies, eds. M. Freeden and M. Stears. Oxford: Oxford University Press.

Halkyard-Harawira, Hilda, and Katie Boanas. 1992. "Pacific Connections: Women and the Peace Movement in Aotearoa." In *Feminist Voices: Women's Studies Texts for Aotearoa/New Zealand*, ed. Rosemary Du Plessis, 317–324. Auckland: Oxford University Press.

Hall, Ian. 2014. "Martin Wight, Western Values, and the Whig Tradition of International Thought." *The International History Review* 36 (5): 961–981.

———. 2015. *Dilemmas of Decline: British Intellectuals and World Politics, 1945–1975*. Berkeley: University of California Press.

Hanchard, Michael. 2018. *The Spectre of Race: How Discrimination Haunts Western Democracy*. Princeton: Princeton University Press.

Heath, Malcolm. 2008. "Aristotle on Natural Slavery." *Phronesis: A Journal for Ancient Philosophy* 53 (3): 243–270.

Heinze, Andrew R. 2003. "Schizophrenia Americana: Aliens, Alienists, and the 'Personality Shift' of Twentieth-Century Culture." *American Quarterly* 55 (2): 227–256.

Henderson, Errol A. 2017. "The Revolution Will Not Be Theorised: Du Bois, Locke, and the Howard School's Challenge to White Supremacist IR Theory." *Millennium* 45 (3): 492–510.

Henry, Devin M. 2007. "How Sexist Is Aristotle's Developmental Biology?" *Phronesis* 52 (3): 251–269.

Hodson, H. V. 1950. "Race Relations in the Commonwealth." *International Affairs* 26 (3): 305–315.

Intondi, Vincent. 2019. "The Dream of Bandung and the UN Treaty on the Prohibition of Nuclear Weapons." *Critical Studies on Security* 7 (1): 83–86.

Inayatullah, Naeem, and David L. Blaney. 2004. *International Relations and the Problem of Difference*. New York: Routledge.

Jackson, Mark. 2018. *Coloniality, Ontology, and the Question of the Posthuman*.

Jacobs, Robert. 2013. "Nuclear Conquistadors: Military

Colonialism in Nuclear Test Site Selection during the Cold War." *Asian Journal of Peacebuilding* 1 (2): 157–177.

Junger, Sebastian. 2019. "Our Politics Are in Our DNA. That's a Good Thing." *Washington Post*, July 5, 2019. https://www.washingtonpost.com/opinions/our-politics-are-in-our-dna-thats-a-good-thing/2019/07/05/c4d8579e-984d-11e9-830a-21b9b36b64ad_story.html.

Kant, Immanuel. 1991a. "Conjectures on the Beginning of Human History." In *Kant: Political Writings*, ed. H. S. Reiss, 221–234. Cambridge: Cambridge University Press.

———. 1991b. *The Metaphysics of Morals*. Cambridge: Cambridge University Press.

———. 2010. "Observations on the Feeling of the Beautiful and Sublime." In *Anthropology, History and Education*, eds. G. Zöller and R. B. Louden, 18–62. Cambridge: Cambridge University Press.

———. 2011a. "Determination of the Concept of a Human Race." In *Kant: Anthropology, History, and Education*, eds. Robert B Louden and Günter Zöller, 143–159. Cambridge: Cambridge University Press.

———. 2011b. "Of the Different Races of Human Beings." In *Kant: Anthropology, History, and Education*, eds. Robert B Louden and Günter Zöller, 82–97. Cambridge: Cambridge University Press.

Keelan, Teorongonui Josie, and Christine Woods. 2006. "Māuipreneur: Understanding Māori Entrepreneurship." *International Indigenous Journal of Entrepeneurship, Advancement, Strategy and Education* 2 (2). http://www.indigenousjournal.com.

Kevles, J. Daniel. 1985. *In the Name of Eugenics: Genetics and the Uses of Human Heredity*. New York: Knopf.

Kissinger, Henry A. 1960. "Limited War: Conventional or Nuclear? A Reappraisal." *Daedalus* 89 (4): 800–817.

Kohn, Margaret, and Daniel I. O'Neill. 2006. "A Tale of Two Indias: Burke and Mill on Empire and Slavery in the West Indies and America." *Political Theory* 34 (2): 192–228.

Labat, Jean-Baptiste. 1724. *Memoires Des Nouveaux Voyages Faits Aux Isles Françoises*. Vol. 2. Haye.

Larrimore, Mark. 2008. "Antinomies of Race: Diversity and Destiny in Kant." *Patterns of Prejudice* 42 (4–5): 341–363.

Las Casas, Bartolomé de. 1997. "Apologetic History of the Indies." http://www.columbia.edu/acis/ets/CCREAD/lascasas.htm.

Latham, Michael E. 2010. *The Right Kind of Revolution: Modernization, Development, and U.S. Foreign Policy from the Cold War to the Present.* Ithaca: Cornell University Press

Leonard, Thomas C. 2017. *Illiberal Reformers: Race, Eugenics, and American Economics in the Progressive Era.*

Lugard, F. D. 1922. *The Dual Mandate in British Tropical Africa.* Edinburgh; London: W. Blackwood and Sons.

Macmillan, John. 2013. "Intervention and the Ordering of the Modern World." *Review of International Studies* 39 (5): 1039–1056.

Malinowski, Bronislaw. 1929. "Practical Anthropology." *Africa: Journal of the International African Institute* 2 (1): 22–38.

———. 1945. *The Dynamics of Culture Change.* New York: Yale University Press.

———. 1954. *Magic, Science and Religion: And Other Essays.* Garden City, N.Y: Doubleday.

Malkin, Irad. 2004. "Postcolonial Concepts and Ancient Greek Colonization." *MLQ: Modern Language Quarterly* 65 (3): 341–364.

Malthus, Thomas Robert. 1798. *An Essay on the Principle of Population.* London: J. Johnson.

Mazower, Mark. 2009. *No Enchanted Palace: The End of Empire and the Ideological Origins of the United Nations.* Princeton: Princeton University Press.

McKittrick, Katherine. 2015. *Sylvia Wynter: On Being Human as Praxis.* Durham: Duke University Press.

Merriam, Charles E. 1926. "Progress in Political Research." *The American Political Science Review* 20 (1): 1–13.

Mignolo, Walter, and Catherine E Walsh. 2018. *On Decoloniality: Concepts, Analytics, and Praxis.*

Naidu, Vijay. 1986. "The Fiji Anti-Nuclear Movement:

Problems and Prospects." presented at the United Nations University Conference, Auckland.

Neocosmos, Michael. 2014. "The Mandé Charter of 1222." *The Frantz Fanon Blog* (blog). November 29, 2014. http://readingfanon.blogspot.com/2014/11/the-mande-charter-of-1222.html.

Nesbitt, Nick. 2014. "Resolutely Modern: Politics and Human Rights in the Mandingue Charter." *The Savannah Review*, no. 4: 11–19.

Nishitani, Osamu.. 2006. "Anthropos and Humanitas: Two Western Concepts of Human Being." In *Translation, Biopolitics, Colonial Difference*, eds. Naoki Sakai and Jon Solomon, 259–274. Hong Kong: Hong Kong University Press.

Oppenheim, Lassa. 1920. *International Law: A Treatise*, ed. Ronald F. Roxburgh. 3rd edn. Vol. 1. New Jersey: Lawbook Exchange, Ltd.

O'Reilly, Kenneth. 1997. "The Jim Crow Policies of Woodrow Wilson." *Journal of Blacks in Higher Education*, no. 17: 117–121.

Pye, Lucian W. 1958. "The Non-Western Political Process." *Journal of Politics* 20 (3): 468–486.

———. 1965. "The Concept of Political Development." *The ANNALS of the American Academy of Political and Social Science* 358 (1): 1–13.

Raz, Mical. 2013. *What's Wrong with the Poor? Psychiatry, Race, and the War on Poverty*. Chapel Hill: University of North Carolina Press.

Roberts, Neil. 2015. *Freedom as Marronage*. Chicago: University of Chicago Press.

Rodney, Walter. 1968. "Education and Tanzanian Socialism." In *Tanzania: Revolution by Education*, ed. Idrian N. Resnick, 71–84. Arusha: Longmans of Tanzania Ltd.

———. 1989. *How Europe Underdeveloped Africa*. Nairobi: Heinemann Kenya.

Rosenau, James N, and Ernst-Otto Czempiel. 1992. *Governance Without Government: Order and Change in World Politics*. Cambridge: Cambridge University Press.

Sabaratnam, Meera. 2016. *Decolonizing Intervention:*

International Statebuilding in Mozambique. London: Rowman & Littlefield International.

Salkever, Stephen G. 2014. *Finding the Mean: Theory and Practice in Aristotelian Political Philosophy*. Princeton University Press.

Santos, Boaventura de Sousa. 2013. *Epistemologies of the South: Justice against Epistemicide*. Boulder: Paradigm Publishers.

Satterfield, Terre, Mere Roberts, Mark Henare, Melissa Finucane, Richard Benton, and Manuka Henare. 2005. "Culture, Risk and the Prospect of Genetically Modified Organisms as Viewed by Tāngata Whenua." https://scholarsbank.uoregon.edu/xmlui/bitstream/handle/1794/20637/558.pdf?sequence=1&isAllowed=y.

Saul, John S. 2010. *Revolutionary Traveller: Freeze-Frames from a Life*. Winnipeg: Arbeiter Ring.

Saull, Richard. 2005. "Locating the Global South in the Theorisation of the Cold War: Capitalist Development, Social Revolution and Geopolitical Conflict." *Third World Quarterly* 26 (2): 253–281.

Selassie I, Haile. 1963. "Towards African Unity." *Journal of Modern African Studies* 1 (3): 281–91.

Shell, Susan. 2001. "Kant's Observations on the Feeling of the Beautiful and the Sublime." *Political Science Reviewer* 30: 34–57.

Shils, Edward. 1960. "Political Development in the New States." *Comparative Studies in Society and History* 2 (3): 265–292.

Shivji, Issa G. 1993. *Intellectuals at the Hill: Essays and Talks 1969-1993*. Dar es Salaam: Dar es Salaam University Press.

Somit, Albert. 1972. "Review Article: Biopolitics." *British Journal of Political Science* 2 (2): 209–238.

Spencer, Herbert. 1852. "A Theory of Population." *The Westminster Review* 1 (II): 468–501.

Sukarno, Ahmed. 1955. "Speech by President Soerkarno at the Opening of the Asian-African Conference, April 18th, 1955." In *The Asian-African Conference*, ed. Walter Kahlin, 39–51. Ithaca: Cornell University Press.

Tate, Merze, and Doris M. Hull. 1964. "Effects of Nuclear

Explosions on Pacific Islanders." *Pacific Historical Review* 33 (4): 379–393.

Teaiwa, Teresia K. 1994. "Bikinis and Other s/Pacific n/ Oceans." *The Contemporary Pacific* 6 (1): 87–109.

Thakur, Vineet, and Peter C. J Vale. 2020. *South Africa, Race and the Making of International Relations*. London: Rowman & Littlefield International.

Thiong'o, Ngũgĩ wa. 1986. *Decolonising the Mind: The Politics of Language in African Literature*. Nairobi: Heinemann.

Trivellato, Francesca. 2010. "Renaissance Italy and the Muslim Mediterranean in Recent Historical Work." *Journal of Modern History* 82 (1): 127–155.

Tuplin, Christopher. 1985. "Imperial Tyranny: Some Reflections on a Classical Greek Political Metaphor." *History of Political Thought* 6 (1/2): 348–375.

Turco, R. P., O. B. Toon, T. P. Ackerman, J. B. Pollack, and Carl Sagan. 1983. "Nuclear Winter: Global Consequences of Multiple Nuclear Explosions." *Science* 222 (4630): 1283–1292.

Tuschman, Avi. 2013. "Can Your Genes Predict Whether You'll Be a Conservative or a Liberal?" *The Atlantic*, October 24, 2013. https://www.theatlantic.com/politics/ archive/2013/10/can-your-genes-predict-whether-youll-be-a-conservative-or-a-liberal/280677/.

Vitalis, Robert. 2015. *White World Order, Black Power Politics: The Birth of American International Relations*. Ithaca: Cornell University Press.

Vought, Hans. 1994. "Division and Reunion: Woodrow Wilson, Immigration, and the Myth of American Unity." *Journal of American Ethnic History* 13 (3): 24–50.

Wallerstein, Immanuel. 1997. "The Unintended Consequences of Cold War Area Studies." In *The Cold War and the University: Toward an Intellectual History of the Postwar Years*, eds. Noam A. Chomsky, Ira Katznelson, and Richard C Lewontin, 195–231. New York: New Press.

Ward, Julie K. 2002. "Ethnos in the Politics: Aristotle and Race." In *Philosophers on Race: Critical Essays*, eds. Tommy L. Lott and Julie K. Ward. Oxford: Blackwell.

Watson, James. 2010. "The Origin of Metic Status at Athens." *The Cambridge Classical Journal* 56: 259–278.

Watson, John B. 1913. "Psychology as the Behaviorist Views It." *Psychological Review* 20 (2): 158–77.

———. 1924. *Behaviorism*. New York: W.W. Norton.

Weber, Heloise. 2007. "A Political Analysis of the Formal Comparative Method: Historicizing the Globalization and Development Debate." *Globalizations* 4 (4): 559–572.

Whyte, Kyle Powys. 2017. "Our Ancestors' Dystopia Now: Indigenous Conservation and the Anthropocene." In *The Routledge Companion to the Environmental Humanities*. London: Routledge.

Wight, Martin. 1936. "Christian Pacificism." *Theology* 33: 12–21.

———. 1946. *Power Politics*. London: Royal Institute of International Affairs.

———. 1966a. "Western Values in International Relations." In *Diplomatic Investigations*, eds. E. H. Butterfield and M. Wight, 89–131. London: Allen & Unwin.

———. 1966b. "Why Is There No International Theory?" In *Diplomatic Investigations*, eds. E. H. Butterfield and M. Wight, 17–34. London: Allen & Unwin.

———. 1972. "International Legitimacy." *International Relations* 4 (1): 1–28.

Wilson, Woodrow. 1887. "The Study of Administration." *Political Science Quarterly* 2 (2): 197–222.

Young, Robert. 2008. *The Idea of English Ethnicity*. Maiden, MA: Blackwell.

Wilson, Peter. 2004. "Manning's Quasi-Masterpiece: The Nature of International Society Revisited." *The Round Table* 93 (377): 755–769.

Wynter, Sylvia. 1968. "We Must Learn to Sit Down Together and Talk About a Little Culture: Part One." *Jamaica Journal* 2: 23–32.

———. 1984. "New Seville and the Conversion Experience of Bartolome de Las Casas." *Jamaica Journal* 17 (2): 25–32.

———. 1991. "Columbus and the Poetics of the Propter Nos." *Annals of Scholarship* 8 (2): 251–286.

———. 2001. "Towards the Sociogenic Principle: Fanon, Identity, the Puzzle of Conscious Experience, and What It Is like to Be 'Black.'" In *National Identities and Sociopolitical Changes in Latin America*, eds. Mercedes F. Durán-Cogan and Antonio Gómez- Moriana, 30–66. New York: Routledge.

———. 2003. "Unsettling the Coloniality of Being/Power/ Truth/Freedom: Towards the Human, After Man, Its Overrepresentation – An Argument." *CR: The New Centennial Review* 3 (3): 257–337.

———. 2015. "The Ceremony Found: Towards the Autopoetic Turn/Overturn, Its Autonomy of Human Agency and Extraterritoriality of (Self-)Cognition." In *Black Knowledges / Essays in Critical Epistemology*, ed. Sabine Broeck, 184–252. Liverpool: Liverpool University Press.

Index